I0027900

fOSLA

Frustrated One-Sided
Lovers' Association

Pradeep Kapoor did his schooling from The Scindia School, Gwalior. He was the topper of his batch in the MBBS course. After completing his MD in paediatrics, he worked in various organizations before starting private practice. He is not a prude who won't admit that he enjoyed reading James Hadley Chase and Louis L'Amour as a youngster. *Papillon* by Henri Charrière, *Roots* by Alex Haley, and *Exodus* by Leon Uris are some of his favourite books.

By the same author:

Commonsense Parenting
co-authored with Neelkamal Kapoor

Make Your Child a Winner

101 Health Problems of Children

fOSLA

Frustrated One-Sided Lovers' Association

Loving and Living in a Medical College

Pradeep Kapoor

RUPA

Published by
Rupa Publications India Pvt. Ltd. 2012
7/16, Ansari Road, Daryaganj
New Delhi 110002

Sales Centres:

Allahabad Bengaluru Chennai
Hyderabad Jaipur Kathmandu
Kolkata Mumbai

ISBN: 978-81-291-2060-1

10 9 8 7 6 5 4 3 2 1

The moral right of the author has been asserted.

Typeset in Adobe Jenson Pro 11/13.9

Printed at Repro Knowledgecast Limited, India

This book is dedicated to my best friend, Neelkamal, who also happens to be my wife. When your life partner is also your partner in life, 'zindagi' becomes beautiful. Thank you my in-house Google search engine for finding answers to all difficult questions life poses and re-poses.

Contents

MBBS

First Professional
Duration 12 months

Subjects:
1. Anatomy
2. Physiology
3. Biochemistry

Second Professional
Duration 18 months

Subjects:
4. Pathology
5. Pharmacology
6. Microbiology
7. Forensic Medicine

Final Professional

Part 1
(Junior Final)
Duration 12 months

Subjects:
8. ENT
9. Ophthalmology
10. Community Medicine

Part 2
(Senior Final)
Duration 12 months

Subjects:
11. Medicine
12. Surgery
13. Obstetrics and Gynaecology

What is FOSLA?

GENESIS: What do you do if the college is teeming with beautiful girls? Simple, you fall for them. But actually, it's not that uncomplicated. The girls are not there to cater to your androgenic drive. Most don't even bat an eyelid as boy after boy goes down. This creates the FOSLA, which is omnipresent but is especially strong in medical colleges.

Foslas or Frustrated One-Sided Lovers' Associations exist in all colleges. Medical college FOSLAs are thriving bodies with large memberships, probably because there is an abundance of girls. All the FOSLA members have faced rejection at the hands of girls at some time or the other. This leads to intense frustration, therefore FOSLA members are also called 'frustoos'. FOSLAs are the exclusive domain of jilted males, girls being too rational to fall in this trap. The members usually greet each other shouting, '*Abey, Fosley, kya chal raha hai?*' or 'Hi, buddy, what's up?'

This is what FOSLA is all about:

- FOSLA members are living examples of optimism and the never-say-die spirit. They operate on the premise: '50 per cent *baat pakki hai,*' that is, from their side.
- The remaining 50 per cent depends on the girl they aim to hook up with, because if the girl says no, their 50 per cent also gets nullified.
- They work tirelessly towards achieving their objective,

unmindful of the kicks on their butts. They incur several expenses during these endeavours like buying branded clothes and shoes, keeping flashy mobiles and treating classmates in swanky joints (the precondition for this practice is that the girls they are angling to hook must be a part of the group). These expenses are passed on to their parents as money supposedly well spent on books and other medical paraphernalia.

- The male partner exercises a firm control over his 50 per cent share (not allowing others to even talk to the girl he wants to hook up with).
- The female counterpart has a 50 per cent stake, but is totally unaware of the whole thing.
- The share-brokers (batchmates and seniors with designs on the girl) and other minimally involved guys—because no guy is uninvolved where girls are concerned—laugh away to glory.

How to recognize a frustoo:

Take the following test and if you score more than seven you are a certified frustoo.

Favourite Saint: St Valentine

Favourite Date: 14 February

Favourite Movie: *Pyaar Ka Panchnama*

Favourite pastime: Discussing the female anatomy (but still failing in anatomy practicals)

Favourite hangouts: Malls, multiplexes and bus stops near girls' colleges

Favourite book: Not applicable

Feared festival: Raksha Bandhan

Frequent fantasy: Licking an ice cream cone together with the dream girl

Frequent injury: 'Bird' hit

Girls ke side effects: Drooling, tachycardia (rapid heart rate), excitement and/or agitation, difficulty in breathing

The shair or couplet most apt for FOSLA members:

Pyaar kismet hai koi khwab nahi,
Ye woh khel hai jisme sabhi kamyab nahi…
Jinhe ishq ki panah mili woh chand log hain
Aur jinki aisi-ki-tasi ho gayi unka hisab nahi

Love is luck, not a dream
This is a game where few succeed
Those who find love are lucky indeed
Thousands who get screwed, help they need

Prologue

When Jai Dhawan, JD to friends, cracked the CPMT (Central Pre-Medical Test), all he could think of was the pretty medico girls sashaying down the medical college corridors in tight jeans and tighter tops. Just like the dream colleges in the umpteen Bollywood flicks he had devoured during his adolescence. His rank in the merit list got him into Nehru Medical College, Bhopla. And boy, was he ready!

When JD cleared the CPMT, it was as much news as Virendra Sehwag hitting a boundary. At his school, DPS (Delhi Public School), Mathura Road, all the teachers were sure that he would get through. After all, JD had outscored every single student in every single subject in every class. He didn't have to mug up facts and figures—he was a natural. The icing on his academic cake was that he was outstanding in sports too.

Mr Rajendra Dhawan, JD's father, accompanied him to Bhopla to complete the admission formalities and also to help him settle down in the hostel. Although outwardly JD insisted that there was no need for Dad to accompany him and that he was grown up enough to fend for himself, inwardly he was relieved to have his father with him in this transitory phase of his life. The Tamil Nadu Express reached Bhopla at around ten o'clock in the morning and JD had his first glimpse of the town where he was going to spend the next five years of his life. The town of Bhopla didn't impress him at all. On the contrary, it was quite a let-down for a Delhite like JD. The rather dingy railway station and narrow by-lanes through which the autorickshaw took them to the medical college were reminiscent of the chaotic Old Delhi.

All that changed the moment JD set his eyes on the five-storeyed college building. Sitting atop a hillock, it looked quite imposing. JD liked the peach and white combination in which the building was painted. The autorickshaw dropped them in front of the porch where several seniors were lurking behind the pillars, ready to pounce on unsuspecting freshers, especially the one without guardians.

The college building was equally impressive from the inside. From the porch, JD and his father entered the high-domed atrium, which was flanked by broad stairways leading up to various departments. The building had four interconnected blocks—east, west, north and south. A wide corridor ran through them on each floor. On the ground floor in the middle of these blocks was a rectangular courtyard with a badminton court. The college library occupied a major portion of the ground floor, which it shared with the anatomy dissection hall and cadaver storage area.

The dean's office was on the first floor. Alongside it were the offices of the AO (Administrative Officer) and clerical staff looking after establishment work. A small office for student welfare activities was tucked away in one remote corner. Beyond the dean's office, connected by a long winding corridor, was the college auditorium and between the two were the restrooms, their walls splattered with graffiti.

By late afternoon, the admission formalities and hostel allotments were finally completed. JD and Mr Dhawan went to the nearby market and after grabbing a quick meal, did some essential shopping for the hostel life that JD was to begin: a bucket and mug, a liquid vapourizer mosquito-repellent (with an extra refill), a small wall mirror, cloth hangers, a bar of washing soap and some snacks and biscuits to fall back on if hunger pangs struck in the middle of the night. They took an autorickshaw back to the hostel and after spending some more time with JD, Mr Dhawan left for the railway station to catch the Tamil Nadu Express back to Delhi. Even though JD felt a vacuum, an unexplicable emptiness, after his father left, he was so tired that he went off to sleep the moment he hit the bed.

⊕

1

Ragging Woes

Out of the three subjects taught in the first year of the course offered by the medical college, anatomy was probably the toughest, followed by biochemistry. Physiology was the least frightening. The mornings were devoted to theory lectures and the afternoons were reserved for anatomy dissection as well as physiology and biochemistry tutorials and practicals. Anatomy dissection taught with the help of human cadavers preserved in formalin is not everyone's cup of tea. The grotesque faces, the stiff limbs and the shrivelled bodies can unsettle even the toughest of students.

The anatomy dissection hall was a long tunnel-like room with two rows of shiny steel-topped tables. Eight students to a table was the norm, which meant that one cadaver was shared by eight students. The all-pervading pungent smell of formalin can be quite suffocating. One or two weaklings from every batch faint during the first few days, while the others suffer from burning and watering of the eyes and nose. Within a week or two, everyone usually adjusts to the situation and, soon, quite comfortably eats their lunch in the company of cadavers.

JD, along with four other boys and three girls, was allotted table number six in the anatomy dissection hall. The allotment was done in alphabetical order. JD and the other three boys—Junaid Ansari, Lazarus Daniel and Manish Shrivastav—were crestfallen because Mehul Upulkar was allotted a seat on the opposite side of the table along with the three girls, Mansi Manchanda, Minal Patnaik and Mita Varma. Mehul sat plumb in the middle of the ravishing Mansi and the petite Minal. The four members of the aggrieved party felt as if they were sitting in Pakistan across the Line of Control.

God is often unfair in doling out goodies to his subjects. His partiality was quite apparent in the case of JD, whom he had given an unfairly fair complexion, a muscular physique and clean-cut, chiselled features. He was the obvious choice for the title of HLT (Handsome List Topper) of the batch. Mehul was a regular chap, in fact, so regular you sometimes failed to notice him. Junaid was short and fat, Manish was giraffe-like with an uncommonly long neck and a triangular face and Lazarus's broad nose and flared nostrils were wider than his mouth. If JD was fit to be HLT, Mansi was the most deserving candidate for the title of BLT (Beauty List Topper) of the batch. Her flawless complexion, arrestingly beautiful features and curvaceously svelte figure were simply mind-blowing. Minal was charm personified with one-centimetre deep dimples on each cheek and Mita was spectacularly buxom with a moonlike face.

The first few days had been a bit of a dampener for JD. All the girls around him were wrapped demurely in white salwar-kameezes, their figures totally lost in the long aprons they had to wear over their kameezes. He cursed the mandatory dress code for the first-year students. Even he was wearing a white shirt and pants under his apron.

JD was sitting on a tall stool, looking down gloomily at the male cadaver lying on the steel table-top in its full naked glory. Today was his third visit to the dissection hall but the dead body still managed to give him the jitters. On top of it, the pungent smell of formalin made his life difficult. His eyes watered incessantly and his breath came out in short laboured gasps. Each of the assembled students had *Cunningham's Manual of Practical Anatomy* open on the table along with a dissection box containing a scalpel, scissors and forceps placed strategically on display. The girls tried to decipher the medical language of the dissection manual, while the boys were busy mugging the 'notes' provided to them by their dear seniors. The notes contained a college song and a college anthem written by Riyaaz Mamu, a very senior incumbent of NMC (Nehru Medical College), Bhopla. He had been in the college for over twenty years and was still counting the years! Both the song and the anthem were strictly non-vegetarian in nature and only for private consumption.

True to his name, Riyaaz Mamu had a lot of practice in each exam. Had his parents known that Riyaaz would take to his name like a fish to water, they would have given him some other name. He was always forced by his friends and well-wishers to appear in the exams, which he dutifully flunked year after year. He had reached the final year thanks to several of his batchmates joining the teaching staff at the medical college, who felt it was their duty to push him along.

The seniors' notes also contained grooming rules for boys, like having short, well-oiled hair, a clean-shaven look, polished shoes, etc. The suggested 'champu' look and white lab attire made juniors sitting ducks for seniors to identify and rag. The notes instructed the juniors to keep their heads down and to never look above the third shirt button of their seniors. Everything has a flip side. Ragging helped develop bonding between the seniors and juniors. So you never had to pay for your tea or bread pakoda when eating with a senior. You also had protection during street brawls with students of other colleges. And if your intimacy became stronger, free booze was the greatest advantage of this association.

At 2 p.m. sharp, the professor of anatomy, Dr S. S. Das, entered the dissection hall along with his two demonstrators,

S. K. Mishra and K. S. Tiwari. Dr Das was around fifty years old, medium built and dark complexioned with close-cropped hair. The most remarkable thing about him was his dark, piercing eyes. It was rumoured in NMC that his angry stare could make even the cadavers piss. Dr Das went straight to the blackboard and started to draw with both his hands simultaneously. Mishra and Tiwari placed themselves at the back to catch any mischief-makers. What are demonstrators for, after all? Dr Das drew the upper half of the human body along with the two upper limbs. Then he started to draw arteries, veins and nerves on the right upper limb. Finishing quickly, he turned to face the class, his menacing gaze sending a small chill down JD's spine. He explained how to dissect various tissues to expose the important nerves and blood vessels. His deep voice and unhurried manner were not only impressive, but also very easy to comprehend. Concluding his lecture, he gave a curt nod and left the dissection hall. Mishra and Tiwari became active and started to go from table to table, doling out instructions on how to cut open the human cadaver. While some of the boys picked up scalpels and gave the cadaver's skin deep incisions, the rest, especially the girls, kept dithering. Cutting open a human being, even a dead one, does require a lot of gumption.

They were soon joined by a short, fat and balding assistant professor, Dr M. T. Bansal, known for his roving eye that had given him a squint in his right one. Well, that's the official version. It was actually the heel of a female staff member's sandal that was to blame for his ophthalmological problem.

Dr M. T. Bansal came to the table occupied by JD et al. They all stood up and MT sat down on the stool previously occupied by Mansi. He asked her to pick up the scalpel and make a six-inch long incision on the right shoulder of the cadaver. With trembling hands, Mansi plucked the scalpel out of the dissection box.

'Is this how you hold the scalpel, miss? What's your name?' MT asked.

'Mansi.'

'Mansi. Nice name, but I have asked you to hold the scalpel to make an incision. I haven't asked you to behead the dead guy with a knife.'

Manish tried to hold back his laughter.

MT shot him a dangerous glare and continued, 'There should be some difference in the way a budding doctor holds a knife and the manner in which a criminal wields a murder weapon.'

Mansi looked down, her eyes flaring with indignation.

'Now let me show you the correct method,' and with that, MT laid his hand over Mansi's. He went on to complete the dissection holding on to Mansi's hand and even when the job was well and truly over, it took Mansi some pulling and pushing to extricate her hand from the clutches of the awfully helpful assistant professor.

'Bastard,' muttered JD as soon as MT left the table. JD was mighty unhappy as he was already considering Mansi as his territory.

'Harami with a capital H,' resonated Junaid. For him, the handholding episode was a bit disconcerting. Mansi didn't seem to share the boys' annoyance. She was quite used to male attention, which she considered to be a necessary evil, a small price to pay for being beautiful. She flashed a bemused smile at JD and Junaid and picked up her things to leave. The anatomy dissection was always held at the end of the day and after it, everybody started to leave for home or the hostel. In a way it was good that this was the last period, so that after sitting for two hours with the dead, you were allowed to escape from them.

As Mansi was exiting the hall, JD caught up with her, 'Mansi! Your scalpel.'

'Oh thanks! It must have slipped beneath the cadaver.'

'No. To be precise, it was lying below the biceps of the cadaver.' JD gave his most disarming smile, which, unfortunately, slipped like the scalpel and missed its target.

'Why don't we name the fellow instead of calling him a cadaver every time,' said Mansi as Minal, Mita, Junaid, Manish, Lazarus and Manish joined them.

'Let's do it,' echoed Minal. 'How about calling him Gabbar, after the dacoit in *Sholay*?'

'Let's name him Shakal,' interjected Manish.

'He looks exactly like Mogambo,' declared Mansi, referring to an iconic villainous character in a Bollywood film.

With JD backing her, the cadaver was rechristened Mogambo. His original name, the one he carried his entire life, the name with which his loved ones addressed him, was long lost. Any name was better than no name! At least now, eight youngsters would call him Mogambo for one full year, maybe with some warmth, some affection. It didn't matter to him that they would cut him up muscle by muscle, fibre by fibre, nerve by nerve.

When the girls dispersed, Junaid asked JD and Mehul, 'How are you guys coping? I've heard ragging is in full swing in the boys' hostel.' Junaid, Manish and Lazarus lived with their families and didn't face any such problem.

Only the previous night, the seniors had organized an 'Induction Day Parade' in the hostel. All the first-year students had done a nude march-past, wearing only ties around their necks. Three senior students standing on a makeshift platform of plastic chairs took the salute and prodded them to shake their asses more vigorously.

'I am sick of dancing to filmy item songs like "*Munni badnam hui*" and "*Kanta laga*", said JD in an irritated tone.

'And I am tired of being chased around by that black, fatso

Manav Sisodia, with *"Monika, oh my darling"* playing full blast,' lamented Mehul.

'The seniors are planning a striptease tonight,' lamented JD.

A faint smile appeared on Junaid's face, which he tactfully smothered down by wiping his face with a hanky. 'Why don't you both stay at my place? Tomorrow is Sunday so you can come to the college on Monday directly from my home.' Junaid lived in a large ancestral home in the old city area, quite close to the medical college. His father owned a printing press located at a walking distance from their house.

'Or you can come to my place,' offered Lazarus Daniel. His father was an assistant engineer with the PWD (Public Works Department) and his mother worked as a clerk in the Electricity Board. Lazarus's offer didn't find favour because he lived in a government colony some fifteen kilometres from the college.

Manish Shrivastav didn't make any offer because he lived in a small two-bedroom flat in a private society. His father was a DSP (Deputy Superintendent of Police) who would surely have got bigger accommodation in the Police Lines colony, but he didn't want his son to grow up among policemen. He felt that by living with them his son would stop fearing the police. He wanted his son to become a law-abiding citizen and for that some fear of the police, he felt, was necessary. Sound logic!

The promise of delicious non-vegetarian food removed whatever little doubt JD and Mehul had about spending the weekend at Junaid's home. That was the first of many occasions when JD and Mehul went there to devour the delicious mutton biryani and chicken rizala prepared by Junaid's mother. After that there was no stopping them. They didn't wait for the month of Ramzan to celebrate Eid. Mrs Ansari was not only a good cook, but also a very warm-hearted lady and feeding these two eternally hungry hostellers gave her a lot of pleasure.

⊕

Every year, a formal welcome party was organized by the college authorities, which meant an end to ragging. This was true at least for the girls. Smart, outspoken people like Mansi and Minal heaved a sigh of relief since they were repeatedly targeted by senior girls who wanted them to fall in line. Ragging in the girls' hostel was not as riotous and unruly as it was in the boys' hostel. It generally meant being asked to sing double-meaning Bollywood songs, like dancing to Madhuri Dixit's famous '*Dhak-dhak karne laga*' number or acting out a romantic scene with another girl dressed as a boy. But this was not so for the boys, especially those living in the hostel. For them the ragging ended much later and with a lot of fanfare!

2

Mayhem in the First Terminals

Soon, JD and his friends got sucked into the cesspool of studies and exams. The medical curriculum in most Indian medical colleges is so loaded, the subjects so new and the books so alien (most of them written by foreigners, such as *Samson Wright's Applied Physiology*, the *Guyton and Hall Textbook of Medical Physiology*, *Ganong's Review of Medical Physiology* and *Gray's Anatomy*), that most of the time students are left gasping for breath.

Of course, there are the Dev Anand-type fellows who march on singing in the style of this Bollywood star, '*Main jindagi ka saath nibhata chala gaya, har fikr ko dhuain main udata chala gaya*'. The only difference is that instead of five, it takes a multiple of five-year plans for them to earn the MBBS (Bachelor of Medicine and Bachelor of Surgery) degree. In some cases, like Riyaaz Mamu's, it takes even longer!

Preparations were in full swing in the boys' hostel for the first terminals, the examination that generally predicted the eventual 'winners' and 'losers'. If students did well in these exams they not only got merit scholarships throughout the four and a half years of the course leading to graduation, but also climbed up in the esteem of their teachers. Parts of all the three subjects taught in the first year—anatomy, physiology and biochemistry—are covered in these exams and only a lucky few manage to get passing marks. Those who do not mug hard are sure to fail in the exams.

JD had put up a saying just above his study table. It read—
'The greatest waste in the world is the difference between what
you are and what you could have been.' Mehul, his room-mate,
was impressed by JD's all-round abilities. JD could talk about girls
for hours, he could drink three bottles of beer straight and still
remain on his feet, he saw more movies than were released (he
saw some more than once) and still was always the first to raise
his hand in the class, even before the question was completed by
the teacher. Despite being in the boys' hostel, the room was rather
neat and Mehul was the primary reason for this anomaly. JD and
Mehul's sides of the room were a study in contrast. While Mehul
had stuck lots of notes on the wall by the side of his bed, JD
had posters of Shakira, Salma Hayek and Lindsay Lohan on his
side. Beautiful girls probably acted as a tonic for his grey matter.

The anatomy and biochemistry question papers were proof of
the extreme sadistic pleasure some teachers derive from flunking
their students. After both papers, students came out in a daze,
unsure of what was asked in them but sure that they had no
clue about it. The physiology paper was somewhat milder, just
like Dr O. P. Mathur, the head of the Department of Physiology
himself. It restored the students' self-esteem to some degree as
they could answer a few of the questions. But their happiness was
short-lived. The mayhem of the theory papers continued unabated
during the practical exams. They were battered and bruised with
the help of human bones by Dr Das and company during the
anatomy viva voce. After the first terminal, the anatomy staff got
the nickname of the 'D-company'.

Lazarus had mugged up the details of several bones for the
anatomy practical exam. When his name was announced he went
in with confidence writ large over his face. Dr Das handed over
the radius bone (the bone of the upper arm) to him. 'Which
bone is it?'

'Radius, sir.'

'Good. *Yeh kis side ki hai?*' Dr Das asked. Determining whether a bone belongs to the right or left side of the body is given great importance in the anatomy practical exam.

Lazarus looked at the bone intently, shifted it from one hand to another, took in a deep breath and smiled.

'Yes, let's hear it. Which side?' Dr Das growled impatiently.

'Sir, looking at the sheen and shine and especially its weight, I think it's from the north, Punjab side!' Lazarus replied innocently.

Dr Das literally fell off his chair. The two demonstrators S. K. Mishra and K. S. Tiwari guffawed loudly and asked Lazarus to scoot.

Manish Shrivastav went in for his viva voce as Lazarus came out in a daze. As he entered, he wished Dr Das, 'Good morning, sir.'

'It's 2 p.m., so a very good afternoon to you. Pick up the radius bone,' he pointed at the pile of bones lying on the table.

Manish picked up a long bone and held it up between himself and Dr Das.

'So, this is the radius bone?' Dr Das grunted.

'Yes, sir.'

'Isn't it a bit too long to fit in the forearm?'

'The guy might have been tall,' Manish put forward a tentative argument.

'How tall are you?'

'Sir, almost six feet. Five feet eleven inches to be precise,' Manish informed Dr Das proudly.

'Place the bone against your forearm,' commanded Dr Das, leaning forward menacingly.

'Yes, sir.' Manish placed the bone against his forearm. Its lower end went well past his outstretched fingers.

'The guy must have been really tall,' said Dr Das sarcastically.

'Yes, sir,' agreed Manish wholeheartedly.

'Any guess how tall?'

'Close to seven feet, sir.'

'Don't you think Indians who are seven feet tall are a bit uncommon?' Dr Das stared at Manish from above his spectacles.

'It could probably be the radius bone of an African,' stammered Manish.

'Ah, yes. Why not! So according to you, this African might have come all the way to Bhopla to donate his radius. You idiot, the bone you have in your hand is the fibula! It is the leg bone, that is why it is so long and not because it belongs to an African. Get out!'

Standing just behind Dr Das, the two demonstrators, S. K. Mishra and K. S. Tiwari, had been tapping their legs frantically for the past five minutes but Manish hadn't caught the signal and that led to his derailment.

In the physiology practical, each student was asked to prick his or her finger with a lancet and estimate his or her own haemoglobin level, the total red blood cell (TRBC) count and the total and differential white blood cell (WBC) count. Mansi was not keen on piercing her finger herself. She was a bit apprehensive about the pain and kept dithering for a while. The ever gallant JD jumped to her rescue and offered her his 'drop of blood' to let her proceed with the practical exam.

During the checking of the practical notebooks, Professor O. P. Mathur noticed that the blood profiles of JD and Mansi were identical. Both had haemoglobin levels of 15 g/dl, TRBC of 5.2 Lac/mm^3 and a total WBC of 6600/mm^3. Even their differential counts were similar: polymorphs 66 per cent, lymphocytes 30 per cent and eosinophils 4 per cent. He was sure they had cheated, but who was the culprit? So to find out, he called them to his chamber separately, one by one.

'May I come in, sir?' JD's usual gruff voice was like a goat's bleat facing a lion in his den.

'Yes. Show me where you pricked your finger.'

'Here, sir,' JD promptly put out the middle finger of his left hand.

'Okay.' Professor Mathur was a bit disappointed when he saw the red prick mark. He had expected JD to be the culprit. He asked a few related questions and was satisfied with the answers. 'You can go now. Send Mansi Manchanda in.'

To get into her good books, JD warned Mansi that Professor Mathur was checking the lancet prick mark.

'What should I do now?' Mansi asked, panicking.

'Prick your finger, quickly.'

'I can't.'

'Come on, be brave.'

'But I don't have a lancet.'

'Put out your left middle finger,' ordered JD. Before Mansi could comprehend what was happening, JD took out a safety pin from the lapel of his apron and jabbed at her finger.

Mansi cried out in pain as blood started to ooze out from the pierced skin. Before entering Professor Mathur's chamber she wiped her finger clean with her hanky. Professor Mathur was confused on seeing a prominent prick mark on Mansi's finger. 'Remarkable, quite remarkable,' he said, looking at Mansi in bewilderment.

'What, sir?' Mansi asked, leaning forward.

'Nothing much, just that your blood value and Jai Dhawan's are exactly alike.' Professor Mathur was a bit suspicious but being a gentle soul, he decided to give the benefit of the doubt to JD and Mansi. He then proceeded to ask a few questions and on receiving satisfactory answers, let Mansi go. All the while Mansi kept standing demurely, her manner epitomizing innocence.

'That was a close call,' said JD when they met in the corridor after Mansi came out.

'I am going to kill you for this,' Mansi showed him her swollen, red finger.

'But I did it in your interest!'

'I am quite capable of taking care of my interests. And I hate physical damage to my delicate fingers.'

'Show me your finger. I'll suck on it and make it heal in a minute. Don't you watch Hindi movies? The hero and heroine do it all the time.' JD caught hold of Mansi's left hand.

'You stupid moron! The hero doesn't first stab at the heroine's finger and then volunteer to suck her blood. That only happens in Dracula movies,' hissed Mansi, snatching her hand back.

JD was a bit upset at the lost opportunity to establish some physical intimacy with Mansi. He consoled himself with the thought that there would always be a next time. He was secure in the knowledge that he knew several tricks of the trade and any of them might bear fruit. And what a fruit Mansi was—ripe and luscious!

The results of the first terminals were declared one week later. JD had topped in anatomy, Mansi was numero uno in physiology and Sumit Saxena had done his father proud by topping in biochemistry (it was another matter that his father Professor P. K. Saxena happened to be the HOD of biochemistry). All three had also qualified for merit scholarships since they had passed in all the three subjects along with an aggregate of 60 per cent marks. On the other hand, Manish, Junaid and Lazarus, who had slogged hard for these subjects, had failed in all three. Mehul was slightly better off because he had managed to pass in anatomy. Maybe mugging with JD had worked for him!

Conforming to the age-old tradition of the first terminal exam of Nehru Medical College and showing solidarity with Manish,

Junaid and Lazarus, the rest of the class had failed in all the subjects with only a handful scoring in double digits.

Thus, the trial by fire began for JD and his batchmates.

3

Fill the Bottle Challenge

The shock and hurt of the terminals was soon forgotten and the students got busy again with their hectic schedules. Theory lectures, demonstration classes, practical periods, cadaver dissection and seminars kept them busy in the day, while the nights were spent dodging those seniors who had an insatiable appetite for ragging. Manav Sisodia aka Danav, stuck in the final professional for the last two years, was the mastermind of all ragging adventures. The moniker Danav was most befitting for Manav. He was six feet two inches tall and almost a metre wide with an enormous paunch hanging down below his belt. His dark complexion, unkempt greasy hair and pockmarked face added to the scary, Frankenstein-like effect.

One Saturday evening, when JD and Mehul returned from the college, they saw some seniors huddled together in the porch talking animatedly. Danav was addressing another group parked in the common room, which was barely furnished with a few chairs, a sofa with most of its springs sticking out and a television which showed only free-to-air channels during the day—but was hooked to a DVD player during the nights for some 'serious' cinema, which also went by the name of porn. For a change, there was much laughter and bonhomie among the heterogeneous group of seniors. JD and Mehul quietly slunk away to their room on the second floor of the hostel.

'Something is cooking,' said JD, unlocking the room. He kicked off his shoes and sat down on the bed. Mehul slid the latch on the door and slumped down on the chair, consternation writ large on his face.

Shortly, in a few minutes, a powerful kick landed on the door, but the latch held firm. JD and Mehul kept sitting on the bed, not even breathing. This was routine. Any senior passing in front of a junior's room delivered a resounding kick on the door, just for the heck of it and to send a chill down the junior's spine.

'O, *khol oye bhencho*. Open the door!' There was a second, more defiant kick on the door.

'Coming, sir!' JD jack-knifed from the bed and opened the door. Danav was at the door, looking extremely peeved.

'What took you so long to respond?' he snarled, and without waiting for the response declared, 'Tonight we have organized the annual "Fill the Bottle Challenge". With this the ragging ends unofficially, but if you try to act smart your seniors can screw you any time. Come to the hostel rooftop at 9 p.m. sharp.' Danav lumbered off, a leer pasted across his acne-ravaged face.

More than six months had passed since the freshers had joined the campus but the ragging was still going on unabated. The risk of breaking any rules set by the seniors was akin to committing hara-kiri.

JD and Mehul flopped down on their respective beds and tried to take a quick nap before the ordeal. JD woke up with a start because of the stomping and screeching that could be heard from the roof above their room. He looked at his watch: it was 8.45. Mehul was fast asleep, snoring gently. JD opened the door and peered into the corridor. Some juniors were lugging wooden chairs up the stairwell, others were hauling plastic buckets full of water to the roof. Arrangements for the night's carnival were in full swing.

'Wake up,' JD shook Mehul. 'It's almost 9.'

Mehul got up from the bed groggily and reconfirmed the time in his wristwatch. 'Shit, man, I hate all this ragging-shagging.'

'Shut up, if Danav and company hear you, they will include shagging with ragging,' JD joked, trying to ease the tension.

'What about dinner?'

'There's no time for that now. Come on, haul ass, let's not anger Danav by being late.' JD slipped on his flip-flops and left the room. Mehul followed him almost immediately and together they climbed up the stairs to the rooftop.

The hostel rooftop was a huge rectangular area surrounded by a low parapet. Naked bulbs hanging from the pillars of the overhead water tank provided temporary lighting. Several seniors were seated on the chairs drinking beer, cigarettes dangling from their lips. A thick cloud of pungent smoke hung over their heads ominously. Packets of chips, salted peanuts and a variety of other snacks were circulating freely. A small CD player blared out the latest item hit to the best of its minuscule capacity.

JD and Mehul joined the gang of thirty-odd juniors standing in a dimly lit corner of the roof. Remaining invisible was a much safer option under such potentially hazardous circumstances. You never knew which senior had what dirty trick up his sleeve. The questions uppermost in every junior's mind were—What the hell is this 'Fill the Bottle Challenge'? Why are seniors making it such a big deal?

Several plastic buckets in various sizes and colours stood near the parapet and an assortment of mugs and glasses was placed beside them on the floor. Two thick, white lines about three feet apart had been drawn in the well-illuminated area of the roof. Some seniors were collecting empty beer bottles and placing them on one of the two white lines. There seemed to be an unending supply of beer and non-veg jokes.

Suddenly, there was a hush followed by a loud cheer not unlike the one that rises up in the air all over the country when India wins a cricket match. It was for a group of seniors reverently called the 'Gestapo'. This was an exclusive club that had only nine members—seven full members and two associates. The seven full members had cleared the MBBS exams and were in various phases of residency. The two prestigious associate memberships were awarded to two MBBS students for their excellence in studies, sports, dramatics and various other activities (some sane, some insane, some describable, some not). Most of the associate members rose to become full members, so the Gestapo usually consisted of the very best seniors.

Everyone was more than keen to offer his chair and his bottle of beer to the Gestapo. Soon everyone settled down and expectedly, the ragging mastermind Danav Sisodia took charge. He went towards the group of juniors and after staring them down, climbed up the parapet. 'Today we are holding the much awaited "Fill the Bottle Challenge". This is a traditional ragging event held every year on this very roof. The winner of the challenge is awarded the much coveted DM, that is, the Doctorate of Micturition.' A loud roar of appreciative laughter rose from the motley crowd.

Danav let his prominent facial creases deepen still further in what was supposed to be a smile, but the effect was quite grotesque. He started to speak again, 'It's quite simple actually—we empty the beer bottles and you fill them up. You can see the empty beer bottles lined up on one white line. You have to stand on the other and piss into the bottle. As soon as your bottle is full, you are free to go down to your room. Remember to pick up your bottle and throw it in the nullah beyond the parapet on the left side.'

'Drink lots of water!' suggested someone from the crowd helpfully. 'Have fun!' greeted another beer-drenched voice. There was a lot of bonhomie and camaraderie on display, of course fuelled by beer and joints.

The juniors rushed towards the buckets and gulped down glasses full of water. Then they dropped their pants and undies in a heap and rushed to the start line. Stripping had long lost its initial hitch and they were now as comfortable without clothes as the cadavers they dissected.

'It would have helped if we also had beer to drink instead of water,' JD said. Meanwhile, Mehul's hose spurted a weak, unsteady stream that fell all around his bottle.

'This is going to take the entire night and we might still be standing here till daybreak,' lamented Mehul.

JD's bottle finally started to fill up gradually, but it was an excruciatingly slow process. At the end of the first hour, JD's bottle was not even a quarter full and Mehul was still struggling to get his aim right. JD looked around to see how the others were faring. Bhavesh Mehta whose room was in the same wing as JD and Mehul's was going great guns. His bottle was already almost three-quarters full!

'Bhavesh Bhai, kamal kar diya. You're doing great! You should be made the irrigation minister of the state, then we won't have any droughts,' joked JD. Bhavesh was from Kutch, an area with a perennial water shortage.

Bhavesh gave a sly smile. 'I learnt how go about this from my cousin, who is a resident in the department of internal medicine. He asked me to take a Lasix tablet before the event. Apparently, it increases the urine output.'

'Do you have some more tablets?' JD asked.

Bhavesh took out a strip of Lasix tablets from his shirt-pocket and offered it to JD. 'Just take one and pass one to Mehul. Be careful, not a word to anyone or we will be screwed without Vazzaline.'

JD smiled at Bhavesh's perfect mimicry of actor Shahid Kapoor's accent in the ad for Vaseline. Both Mehul and he gulped down a tablet each of Lasix and went off to drink more water. Soon, the bottles started filling up. Of course, Bhavesh won the 'Fill the Bottle Challenge', though JD and Mehul were not far behind.

And that marked the grand finale night of ragging at Nehru Medical College.

4

The Frog Which Didn't Turn Into A Prince

Gradually, the students started to get a hang of the medical subjects. Physiology lectures were turning out to be quite interesting. Learning how the human body works, acts and reacts was quite revealing. Professor O. P. Mathur, HOD of physiology, always took pains to keep in mind the lowest denominator among the students. This made learning a breeze for the upper crust of the freshers. Biochemistry was a big bore as was its HOD, Professor P. K. Saxena. The only redeeming feature about the biochemistry department was the presence of Assistant Professor Dr Chandni. No, that was not her real name. Her actual name was Aasha Asnani, but everyone called her Chandni behind her back. The way she dressed for her lectures, you would believe she was attending a wedding inside the classroom and not delivering a tedious sermon on glucose metabolism or the urea cycle. Human anatomy is as tough as the human body is complex. With hundreds of muscles, bones, nerves, arteries, veins, tissues and organs to remember, the subject became progressively more complicated as the course proceeded. The theory lectures were generally held in the first half of the day while the physiology practical and anatomy dissection was scheduled for the second half, after lunch break.

In a series of ten consecutive lectures, Professor Mathur had already taught students how the muscles and nerves function. Now the extremely charming Dr Kiran Parashar, demonstrator in the department of physiology, was to demonstrate how the muscles and nerves actually work—the exact manner in which the impulse is conducted through the nerve, reaches the muscle, and then how the muscle contracts in response.

Special permission had been obtained from the authorities for animal experiments. A frog was kept in a glass container atop the large wooden table in one corner of the classroom. There was a thick glass lid on the container to prevent the frog from jumping out. The fellow was reasonably well built and was apparently asleep, drugged by its inhalation of chloroform.

Dr Kiran arrived, wearing a bright yellow sari and matching accessories. Her intoxicating perfume was more lethal than the chloroform used on the frog because several boys swooned. She opened the attendance register and started calling out the names of the students. Most of the boys were present, in fact, they outnumbered the girls! This only happened in her class for it is only logical that a beautiful female who is also an excellent teacher would attract the boys like bees to honey.

'Now we will begin today's demonstration,' Dr Kiran announced, closing the register. 'I will dissect the muscle in the hind leg of the frog along with the nerve. Then I'll attach the muscle-nerve piece to this device,' she pointed towards an electric motor mounted with a black drum. 'This drum records the contractions of the muscle when a low-voltage current is passed through the nerve by using a battery.'

Dr Kiran walked up to the table and looked carefully at the frog, which didn't stir one bit. Emboldened, she removed the lid and caught hold of the frog by both its hind legs. She placed the frog in the dissection tray and looked at the class. 'Now, who will assist me in the experiment?'

Several hands went up. Almost all the boys were keen to inhale Dr Kiran's enthralling perfume from close quarters. But she wasn't a novice, after all she had studied in the same medical college. She asked Mansi, sitting in the front row, to come up and assist her.

'When I dissect the muscle and nerve, you must tie it with a thread to this metal stylus,' Dr Kiran instructed Mansi.

'Yes, ma'am,' said Mansi.

The moment Dr Kiran cut its skin to expose the muscle, the drowsy frog opened its eyes, took a mighty leap and landed on top of Mansi's head. She jerked backwards, slipped and fell down on the floor. She let out a terrified wail.

'Come on, get up. You don't have to behave as if a bloodsucking bat has attacked you,' ridiculed Dr Kiran, holding out her hand.

Probably the frog didn't like the derogatory racial remark used by Dr Kiran. It took a second leap and deposited itself between the folds of her sari. Dr Kiran went into a wild, tribal dance mode—jumping, twisting, writhing and flaying her arms wildly. The entire class was in raptures, with everybody jumping around like frogs themselves. The commotion went on for about ten minutes as Mr Frog jumped from table to table and it was only Professor Mathur's arrival that restored order. The story was told and retold over and over again till the entire college had heard a detailed and substantially inflated version of it. It was now common knowledge how shapely Dr Kiran's legs were and how well endowed Mansi was.

⊕

A few days later, Mita celebrated her birthday with her tablemates inside the dissection hall. As they were waiting for other students and teachers to arrive, she took out two paper bags and handed out pastries and hot samosas to everyone.

'I love Black Forest pastries,' said Mansi. 'These are simply divine.'

'The samosas are great, too. I am sure if Mogambo was alive he would have started to drool by now,' declared Junaid. 'Where did you get them from?'

'Narmada Sweets, of course,' replied Mita, pointing at the paper bags.

By now, they all had become so used to the all-pervading stench of formalin-soaked cadavers that they had no qualms about eating pastries and samosas sitting among them. They appeared totally at ease with Mogambo.

'Everybody, quiet,' growled Dr M. T. Bansal, entering the dissection hall. Close on his heels was the duo of demonstrators, S. K. Mishra and K. S. Tiwari.

Dr Bansal addressed the class. 'We are finished with the upper limb, now we will begin dissecting the lower limb. I'll tell you about the important structures to be exposed while dissecting the thigh. Once you have dissected the thigh and seen the structures yourself, you will never forget them in your life.'

He went to the blackboard and started to draw briskly. After finishing, he stopped to look at his handiwork admiringly. 'Always remember, the femoral vein is the innermost, then comes the artery, and the outermost is the nerve,' he said, turning to face the class. 'Just remember the mnemonic—VAN. It doesn't stand for Maruti van, it is for Vein, Artery and Nerve,' he laughed heartily at his feeble joke, but no one in the class responded.

Dr Bansal looked at the class quizzically, a bit disappointed that the students didn't share his sense of humour. 'Remembering this fact will be of great use to you when you go to the clinical side and are required to draw blood from the femoral vein.' Whatever his failings, he had this uncanny knack of giving practical clinical tips, which made his lectures quite interesting.

Dr Bansal and the two demonstrators started to circulate among the tables, handing out instructions about how to dissect the structures in the thigh. Dr Bansal finally ended up at JD's table and as everybody stood up, sat down on Mansi's stool.

'What's your name?' he looked at Junaid.

'Junaid Ansari.'

'Come on, make the incision and be careful, otherwise you will cut the vein, artery and the nerve,' he commanded Junaid.

Junaid picked up his scalpel and bending down slightly gave a tentative incision on the skin of the thigh. The formalin-preserved hide-like skin remained intact. He became nervous and in his anxiety tried again with full force. To everyone's horror the sharp blade of the brand-new scalpel went clean through the vein, artery and nerve. It even sliced the muscles and hit the femur, the thigh bone.

Dr Bansal leapt up from his seat. 'You idiot! You moron, look what you have done! What do you want to prove by chopping off the leg of the cadaver? Are you Genghis Khan?' He was beyond himself with rage and went on shouting incoherently. He grabbed Junaid by his shoulder and literally dragged him away towards Dr S. S. Das's chamber.

Within no time, everyone in the demonstration hall got to know about the radical surgical procedure performed by the budding surgeon, Junaid Ansari. The whole class was in an uproar. Mishra and Tiwari, the two demonstrators, first tried to restore order but soon gave up and joined in the hilarity.

5
The Musical Night

A notice was put up on the college noticeboard a few days later, with the words 'Musical Night' etched in bold black. The seniors started checking out their vocal cords each night by wetting them with rum and cola. Soon the preparations for the Musical Night were in full swing.

This was a much awaited event in the social calendar of Nehru Medical College. It broke the tedium of lectures, demonstrations and surprise tests. There was so much hungama during the event every year that each time the dean and the staff vowed to cancel the next year's event. But there was so much pressure from the student union against omitting it from the calendar that it was held again and with increased levels of rowdiness.

There were the gifted singers, the not-so-gifted and then the utterly atrocious bunch, which far outnumbered the first two groups. Unlike in the popular television talent-spotting show *Indian Idol*, there were no auditions, so anyone and everyone got a chance to climb up on stage and sing on key, off-key or, simply, bray. Remaining there for even a few seconds was the real challenge. Hooting was so vigorous and lusty that it was well nigh impossible to catch even the mukhada, leave alone the antara of any song. This was especially true if a fresher was on the stage. It was a see-saw battle between the staff trying to act as the noise pollution control board, and the unruly students behaving as political hoodlums. The staff won the battles but the students were always victorious in the war.

FOSLA was quite active during the Musical Night. This was a God-sent opportunity for the frustoos to vent their feelings. Mostly they sang love songs in lovelorn voices for their target audience, that is, the girls they wanted to phasao, or hook. Some successful seniors with steady girlfriends sang duets, much to the chagrin and envy of the have-nots.

Mehul put in his name as a participant, and so did Mansi. Mehul had formal training in classical music and was a reasonably good singer. After much deliberation with JD, Junaid and Lazarus, he decided to sing a Hindi film song, 'Papa kehte hain bada naam karega'. He would have much preferred to sing a song with a classical base, but it was considered too big a risk, especially coming from a fresher. Mansi was going to render probably the only English number to be presented at the Musical Night. The song was 'Like a prayer' sung by Madonna. Really, girls—especially the beautiful ones—can get away with anything, even murder, thought Mehul.

Three days before D-day, rehearsals with a professional orchestra in attendance started in the college auditorium. JD decided to accompany Mehul to the rehearsals. The stated reason was to give him moral support and also to give him unbiased feedback. The real reason was to hit on Mansi. Mehul hardly needed any moral support as the ragging season was almost over after the 'Fill the Bottle Challenge'. Most of the seniors had had their fill of the ragging pie and were beginning to get chummy with their juniors and only a handful of 'flops' were still at it. As regards the feedback, JD was hardly in a position to judge a trained singer like Mehul.

Aftab Khan, a highly rated singer from the final professional, was practising the peppy song 'Chahe koi mujhe janglee kahe' with the orchestra. When he shouted 'Yahoo!' in between the lines, his voice gave way and the antara got spoilt. He stopped, looked around and saw JD sitting in the front row of the auditorium. 'Are you also participating in the Musical Night?'

'No, sir. I have just come along with Mehul Upulkar.'

'Come up on the stage and accompany me in the song.'

Unsure of what was expected of him, JD climbed up on stage—which is actually the right thing to do when dealing with a senior. Obey!

'What's your name?'

'Jai Dhawan, JD.'

'Okay, JD, as you already know I will be singing the "*Janglee*" song. All you have to do is to shout "Yahoo!" at the right places. Your cue would be when I pat my left thigh with my left hand. Right?'

'Yes, sir.'

'Try shouting "Yahoo!" two to three times. Give it all you have.'

JD inhaled deeply and using all his lung power shouted 'Yahoo!' to the best of his capacity. The impact was astounding. Everyone stopped talking, the orchestra went silent and the homing pigeons stopped their gutar-goo and started to circle wildly.

'Damn good! It's even better than the original 'Yahoo!' in the song.' Aftab Khan was effusive in his praise. JD looked very pleased. Now he was a part of the Musical Night and what a break it was! Lending support to the last year's winner was like getting a role alongside Bollywood superstar Shah Rukh Khan. There was a buzz the next day among his batch mates: *JD is participating in the Musical Night.*

The first day's rehearsal was over a bit early because the members of the orchestra had to perform in a religious function, a jagrata being held in the Punjabi Bagh area of Bhopla. Dr

Kiran Parashar, the head of the college cultural society, who was overseeing the rehearsal, deputed JD and Mehul to accompany Mansi and the other girls up to the gate of the girls' hostel. Entry beyond that point was a recurring dream that every boy had, but which was never fulfilled.

The girls' hostel was a mere ten-minute walk from the auditorium, but there was a dark, lonely stretch in between, so having two male chaperones wasn't such a bad idea. JD thought it was a brilliant idea and he silently thanked Dr Kiran for coming up with it. As the group started to walk towards the hostel, JD came up beside Mansi. With a full moon up in the cloudless sky, he could see her beautiful face clearly. Her large almond-shaped eyes, sharp aquiline nose, full mouth and a gently sloping chin were a sight to behold. The faint flowery perfume emanating from her sent a gentle shudder down JD's spine.

'You sing really well. "Like a prayer" is my favourite too,' JD had to make a real effort to control his galloping heart.

'Thanks. I think I was off-key in some places, but I can improve,' Mansi smiled sweetly.

JD's heart skipped several beats. Girls don't realize they can give a male a heart attack by smiling ever so sweetly. 'That's because the synthesizer fellow was not as well conversant with the song as he should have been,' JD said as an excuse for beautiful Mansi's not-so-melodious rendition of the song. Beauty is all-conquering—as men know to be a fact, while women are matter-of-fact about it.

'Are you also singing at the Musical Night?' asked Mansi, smiling again.

It almost killed JD. But he survived to live another day, 'No and yes. I just came to give Mehul company—instead I have been roped in by Aftab sir to add a few sound effects to his song.'

'I see.' Mansi kept a straight face although she knew the sound effects JD was so proudly talking about were merely shouting

'Yahoo!' in the song. 'What other singers do you like? I mean, what type of music do you enjoy the most?'

'Oh, I am not that particular. From soft country music to hard rock, I listen to all kinds of stuff. It all depends on my mood. I like Kishore Kumar's spunky old numbers and among the newer lot I like Sonu Nigam, Neeraj Sridhar and Mohit Chauhan.'

'That's quite a wide choice.'

'What about you? What type of songs do you like?' JD asked enthusiastically.

'Ditto! Anything and everything. You know what, my parents sent me to classical music, Kathak and French classes at various stages, but I ended up learning pop, hip-hop and American slang.' This time instead of smiling, Mansi started to laugh and JD joined in.

'What's so funny? What's wrong with you two?' Mehul shouted, looking back over his shoulder. Mansi and JD were so engrossed in their discussion that they had fallen some way behind the group. The thick foliage of the trees lining this stretch of the road obliterated the moonlight altogether and no one could see any one clearly in the darkness.

'Oh, it's nothing. Mansi was telling me how she came to learn to sing so well,' yelled back JD. They started to giggle uncontrollably.

At the hostel gate, Mansi and the girls thanked JD and Mehul. 'See you tomorrow at the audi,' said Mansi with the briefest of smiles, but it was enough for JD's heart to break into bhangra. JD kept looking at the receding figure of Mansi, his eyes pinned to her swaying, jeans-clad butt.

'Come on, you Romeo, let's scoot from here. If by chance any senior sees us standing here we are finished.' Mehul caught hold of JD's arm and spun him around.

'Fuck, yaar. You made me miss the last few seconds' viewing of that peach of a butt.'

'By the way, 'pear' would be a more apt word, you pervert.' Mehul smirked and walked away from the girls' hostel.

JD ran up to him and gave a friendly kick on his rear. 'So Swamy Mehulanandji was also swayed by the swinging pear!' They exchanged a couple of innocuous blows and trotted back to the boys' hostel.

⊕

The next evening, Mehul and Mansi were sitting in the back row of the auditorium behind several other participants awaiting their turn to practise with the orchestra. Aftab was on stage rehearsing *'Chahe koi mujhe janglee kahe'* while JD shouted 'Yahoo!' from behind the curtains. Mehul and Mansi exchanged smiles and rolled their eyes each time JD's voice reverberated in the auditorium. Soon it was Mehul's turn and then after some time, Mansi was on the stage singing Madonna's 'Like a prayer'. There were several oohs and aahs as Mansi crooned, holding the mike in her hand.

After the practice session, Dr Kiran arranged for hot tea and samosas. She probably had paid from her pocket for the treat and it was these little touches that made her quite popular with the students, besides the fact that she was an excellent teacher. JD was waiting with bated breath for the opportunity to accompany Mansi to the girls' hostel again. But by now several seniors had woken up to the fact that the girls would need escorts and were waiting just outside the auditorium to do the honours. When JD and Mehul saw two respected Gestapo members and Danav lurking outside, they quietly slunk away. Dr Kiran was also smart enough to realize that enough volunteers for chaperoning were present. She left the scene without assigning the coveted job to anyone.

The last practice night saw an exponential growth in the number of eager escorts. But the presence of Dr Vijay Khanna, HOD of medicine, and Dr P. R. Tripathi, HOD of surgery, saw the senSEX cool down rapidly. A number of FOSLA members had come to the party but were left high and dry. All they could do to release their frustration was to repeatedly rev up their bike engines before disappearing into the night.

⊕

The Musical Night began at 7 p.m. sharp. The college auditorium was kept under siege by the elite commandos drawn from the most feared staff members of the college. They stood at every vantage point, keeping an eye on the known mischief-makers and habitual hooters. A special task force was keeping vigil in the balcony from where the most disturbance was expected.

Praveen Singh, a diminutive, nondescript junior dressed in low-waisted jeans and a denim jacket was the first singer to go on stage. He did a hesitant namaste and tried to bend the mike down to his height of 5 feet 2 inches. The mike didn't budge and before the mike-wallah could come to his assistance, Praveen stood under the mike, raised his face and started to sing '*Bachna ai haseeno lo mein aa gaya*'. Someone from the crowd shouted, '*Bhago, audi mein langoor aa gaya*'—run, there's a monkey in the auditorium. The crowd burst out laughing. Praveen tried to hold his ground, going on to croak '*Husna ka aashik husna ka dushman apni adaa hai sab se juda*'. Atrocious singing and faulty diction made the crowd holler. Riyaaz Mamu, who was compering the programme, put an arm around Praveen and took him backstage.

The second singer, Janardan Dubey, was also from the junior batch. In spite of everyone telling him that the song '*Sultana, Sultana, mera naam hai Sultana*' was originally sung in female voice, he insisted on singing it. He was hooted down so noisily that he couldn't complete the mukhada. Later, after reaching the hostel, he got nicely thrashed by the seniors for singing such a stupid song.

The next contestant, Ghanshyam Prasad, came on stage. He

had a very dark complexion and crinkly hair. By wearing a spotless white shirt teamed with white pants and a three-inch-wide belt with a shiny stainless steel buckle, he had already cooked his goose. He started '*Arre deewano mujhe pehchano kahan se aayaa mein hu kon*'. His batchmates sang back, '*Dongri gaaon se aaya duniya ka sab se kala Don*'. Everyone cheered, 'Don! Don! Don!'

Some semblance of order was restored by a superlative rendering of '*Papa kehte hai bada naam karega*' by Mehul. There was a lot of clapping and shouts of 'Once more!' Then came Mansi and the sight of her in tight jeans and a frilly top elicited a lot of catcalls and wolf whistles. The FOSLA was witnessing the arrival of a new love icon in the medical college. There was pin-drop silence as Mansi sang 'Like a prayer'. Mostly it was because the crowd was staring at her with mouths agape and not being able to decide what she was singing also contributed to some extent. No one wanted to hoot a beauty singing an English song and be labelled as uncouth, a total ganwaar.

The lull in hooting allowed the frustoos to vent their feelings in the songs like '*Pehli nazar mein kaisa jaadu kar diya*', '*Tere mast mast do nain*' and '*Pee loon tere neeley neeley nainon se shabnam*'. When Prem Arora, the undeclared president of FOSLA (because he had been given the boot by at least a dozen girls), came on stage to sing '*Hame tum se pyaar kitna ye ham nahi janate*', the crowd couldn't take it any more. Wisecracks rang out in the auditorium, the loudest being '*Abe frustoo isi liye to sab bhaag gayeen tujhe ditch mar ke*'. All hell broke loose and there was total chaos for some time.

Several staff members launched active patrolling to catch the culprits. One or two miscreants were evicted and others threatened with dire consequences in the forthcoming exams. As the noise level went down, some more bravehearts went on stage and departed from the stage in quick succession. Seizing the opportunity, Riyaaz Mamu unleashed Aftab Khan, Reshmi

Khanna and other established singers. Aftab sang the evergreen *'Chahe koi mujhe janglee kahe'* with JD shouting 'Yahoo!' at the proper places. The crowd simply loved it. Reshmi's rendition of *'Janam samjha karo'* was not a patch on the original sung by Asha Bhonsle, but still much better than the torture the students had suffered so far. Everybody settled down to listen to some soulful music when senior staff members came up on the stage to sing old songs from the Mukesh-Mohammad Rafi era. Dr Seema Banerjee, HOD of gynaecology, sang her favourite *'Aayega, aayega, aayega aane wala'* from the film *Mahal* in her trademark vibrating voice quite akin to the bleating of a she-goat. A spinster touching sixty, she still had not lost hope in her musical abilities.

The Musical Night ended with the declaration of the best male and female singers. The dean, Dr S. L. Gupta, came up to do the honours. He was a short, fidgety man with a shiny, bald pate. The bright spotlights made his takkal appear like a blazing sun on a hot June afternoon. 'The best male singer award goes to...' he paused for effect. The poor fellow was clearly affected by the dime-a-dozen award shows that clutter the television sets. 'Mehul Upulkar!' he announced in a loud cheerful voice. There was loud clapping, specially from the balcony where the juniors were sitting. Dr Gupta peered at the result card in his hand and said, 'And the best female singer award goes to...' he stopped again, quite enjoying the moment, 'Reshmi Khanna!' He almost blurted out—daughter of Dr Vijay Khanna, HOD of medicine. If not for her singing, Reshmi certainly deserved the award for being BLT of her batch. With her Aishwarya Rai eyes on a Sushmita Sen face, she was considered sizzling hot by not only the students, but probably even the cadavers lying in the anatomy dissection hall. Of course, an HOD father is always an asset. Loud catcalls and shrill whistles following the announcement were a clear indication of the huge fan base in FOSLA that Reshmi commanded.

6

Notes-Worthy

'How are your studies getting on?' JD cornered Mansi as she came out of the anatomy lecture hall one day. It was almost a month since that night when they had talked so freely en route to the girls' hostel.

'Okay,' Mansi smiled. JD's heart accelerated to about 150 beats per minute. Oh these girls, what they can do to your adrenalin levels, he thought. 'You know how it is in the hostel, with so many disturbances all the time.'

'Yeah. It's even worse in the boys' hostel,' said JD.

Both were trying to mislead each other—after all they were competitors. In reality things were quite the opposite. The hostel wing populated by first-year professional students was almost quiet these days. The PU (pre-university) exams were due shortly, to be followed by the university exams after a gap of three weeks. Even the seniors did not disturb the midnight-oil burners, because they, too, had gone through similar exam pangs.

'Do you prepare your own notes or just underline important passages in the textbooks?' asked Mansi, curious to know how JD studied.

'Both. Some chapters in some books are written so well that there is no point making notes. That's a waste of precious time. But just try reading about carbohydrate metabolism or the endocrine system in the books and you are stumped.'

'Have you made notes on the endocrine system?' queried Mansi, keeping her tone casual.

'Yes. Full and final.' JD regretted his words the moment they slipped from his mouth. Girls can make fools of the brightest studs, a fact that is strange but true!

'Can you please lend them to me for a day or two? I can't seem to get the hang of so many endocrine glands and their hormones.' Mansi gave JD her most alluring smile.

All the hormones circulating in JD's blood went haywire, especially testosterone. Even though he knew he was committing a grave mistake, he said yes to Mansi. Oh boy, he said to himself, what a sucker he was!

'Hey you two, want to come to the canteen?' Mehul called out. He, Lazarus, Mita and Minal had just emerged from the classroom.

'Sure,' JD and Mansi echoed in tandem.

'Where are Laurel and Hardy?' JD lobbed a question in the air. He was asking about Manish and Junaid.

'They have gone to the library to study for the PUs,' Lazarus volleyed back.

'Let's check them out after we've had tea,' JD declared.

The group walked past the dean's office, down the cavernous corridor to the college canteen situated just above the mortuary. The canteen was a noisy and brightly lit, cheerful place. There were two rows of five tables, each and every conceivable type of chair, and also some stools to sit on. There were different types of chairs, not because of an interior designer's input, but rather, as a cost-saving exercise. The table-tops were artistically engraved with the names of various girls and boys, indicating who supposedly was romantically linked to whom. The 'artwork' of hearts and plus signs speaking of imaginary affairs on the campus. The menu on any given day was tea, coffee, cold drinks, ice cream, samosas, vegetable patties and cream rolls, with South Indian items making an appearance on Wednesdays and Saturdays.

Maheen Pahalwan, whose only passions were bodybuilding and jokes, ran the canteen. He was tall and reed-like, with not a single muscle in his body to speak of, though his name suggested otherwise. His red, paan-stained lips and deep, kohl-smeared eyes made him appear like a very authentic scarecrow. No one knew his real name and he, too, probably had forgotten it by now. Earlier, he had acquired a shady BA degree through a correspondence course and now introduced himself as M. Pahalwan, BA, 'piropriter' of the medical college canteen.

'Maheen Bhai, six special chai,' JD ordered, entering the canteen. The canteen was not too crowded; there was only a smattering of permanent fixtures who attended college from the confines of the college canteen and a few FOSLA activists feeding large chunks of ice cream to whomever they were in love with. Going by the current trends, the love angles were probably triangles, if not quadrangles, with two or more boys often chasing the same girl.

'Six pesal chai,' Maheen Bhai transferred the order to his assistant, Sajju Phukki. Sajju Phukki was a reformed pickpocket who had finally given up on his art after being beaten black and blue by the crowd at a political rally. Had he known the crowds in such rallies were hungrier and meaner than other people, he wouldn't have tried to pick the pocket of a slogan-shouting hoodlum. He suffered a fractured tibia and was left with a permanent limp. It also severely compromised his ability to dash off with the booty he managed to pinch from pockets. Since Maheen Bhai had a reformist streak, he had taken Phukki under his wings.

'Pesal chai.' Phukki placed the tray containing six cups on the table occupied by JD and company. The cups were cunningly designed to give the appearance of more volume. Due to their sharply tapering lower half they had a capacity of not more than 50 ml and it took exactly three and half sips to finish the contents

After finishing his tea, JD went to the counter to pay the bill. 'Maheen Bhai, what were you doing in the hostel last night?'

'Oh, there was a party in room 69. Manav Sisodia had asked me to provide butter chicken and rumali rotis.'

'But you didn't go back until midnight.'

'They were watching a filam and requested me to stay for some time,' Maheen Bhai immediately regretted his mistake in admitting this by biting his tongue.

'Which filam?' JD mimicked Maheen Bhai.

'I don't know.'

'Come on, don't lie. You were watching a blue film.' JD grinned meaningfully.

'Miyan, aapki kasam, I did watch it, but with hatred in my eyes.' Maheen Bhai raised his hands and tugged forcefully at his earlobes.

JD burst out laughing. What a novel way of absolving oneself, this was the height of ingenuity. 'Okay, how much for the tea?'

'Sir, what are you talking about? Where is the money going? Nowhere. Just give me your blessings.'

JD went back to the table, still laughing wildly. 'Maheen Bhai is just too much.'

'Will you tell us what happened or keep laughing like a madman?' Mansi asked, somewhat irritated.

'Yes, but outside the canteen. Maheen Bhai has just bribed me by not charging for the tea. I'll have to keep mum in his presence.'

Everyone choked with laughter when JD repeated his conversation with Maheen Bhai on the way to the library.

It was in this state that they entered the library, where another shocker awaited them. Junaid and Manish were closeted in a corner poring over *Gray's Anatomy*, a thick tome of over one thousand pages. Lazarus came over and looked at them in total amazement. 'What are you guys doing?'

'We are studying the chapter on the brain in *Gray's Anatomy*,' replied Junaid in all seriousness.

'Do you have that much of a brain? You morons, even toppers don't do that. Go pick up *R. D. Chaurasia*, otherwise you will flunk the exams.' Lazarus was aghast.

JD came over and surveyed the scene. 'Yes, what Lazarus is saying is right. Even I don't study directly from *Gray's*. I have prepared my notes and have collected some seniors' notes too. I mostly study from Indian books.' The fact of the matter is that most popular medical books are written by foreign authors. Of late, however, Indian books of quite a high standard have arrived on the scene, and are well accepted by students because they are relatively easy to comprehend. By and large, reading habits in medical colleges are influenced by the seniors, some of who donate their expensive books while others dispense their advice free of charge.

Mansi went to the physiology section to look for the *Guyton Textbook*. She wanted to study the complex chapter on muscles and nerve conduction in it. The seniors in the hostel had advised her that Guyton had described this topic very lucidly, but she could not find it. She looked for *Ganong's*, another tome. Seeing it on the top shelf she took it to the librarian to get it issued. 'Come, let's hurry. Dr Kiran's special tutorial class starts at 2 p.m. She will cover all the important topics,' said Minal urgently, looking at her watch. They all trouped out of the library and went upstairs to the second floor where the physiology demonstration hall was situated.

JD allowed himself a small smile. He was holding on to the *Guyton and Hall Textbook of Medical Physiology* for almost a month now and was planning to keep it with him till the final exams were over. Later, he would pay up the fine. These little tricks were all part of the game.

⊕

The PU exams began on a dark, cloudy Monday morning and ended on an equally bleak Saturday afternoon. The performance of the students was bleaker with even the 'stars' of the batch failing to shine. Only the star-studded Indian cricket team can put up such a pathetic show.

Besides JD, Mansi, Sumit Saxena and two others, none of the 150 students could pass in all the three subjects. Even these five barely scraped through. About 10 per cent managed to pass in two subjects, 20 per cent got through in just one and the remaining 70 per cent failed in all the three subjects. Laurel and Hardy (Manish and Junaid), as usual, believed in going with the majority.

Just as South Africa, England and Australia prepare green, bouncy pitches to clean bowl our hapless cricketers, the anatomy, physiology and biochemistry departments routed the wretched students with their cannonball questions. This was an old trick used by the teachers to jolt the students out of their lethargy. According to them, it was a good warming-up exercise, motivating the students to put in fourteen to sixteen hours of concerted hard work in the intervening three weeks before the final exams. A vast majority managed to pass the exams just because of this time-tested formula.

Forgetting the mauling they had received in the PUs, the students started to study really hard. JD barely left his room, except in the evenings to take a brief stroll. Somehow, most students start feeling an acute need for such refreshing pastimes during the exams. Then there are chaps whose bhakti erupts during this period, when they can be seen visiting various temples lighting incense and drinking holy water. Otherwise, when the exams are a safe distance away, their visits are restricted to malls, multiplexes and the gates of various girls' colleges.

During one such evening walk, JD passed by the girls' hostel. No self-respecting alpha male can restrain himself from checking out the girls adorning various windows and balconies of the hostel and JD was no different. He stopped in his tracks, as he spotted Mansi waving at him from the third-floor balcony of her room. All hostels, across India, generally have this straightforward rule—juniors stay on the sun-baked top floor and seniors get to enjoy the coolness of the ground floor. JD waved back with his right hand and thumped his chest with the left to reverse the cardiac arrest he had just suffered. He remained stationary in front of the hostel gates. Mansi was down in two minutes flat, her chest heaving with unaccustomed physical exertion. The red flush on her cheeks accentuated her devastating beauty.

'I wanted to return your notes and also say a sincere thank you. They really helped, otherwise I would have flunked the physiology exam,' she said breathlessly.

JD was too overwhelmed by this chance meeting with Mansi. He was tongue-tied and just kept devouring her with his eyes, not saying a word. 'Hey, is anything wrong?' asked Mansi.

'No, everything is just great.' JD finally found his voice. He took a deep breath to control his excitement.

'You appear pale. Are you studying too hard?'

'No, I'm doing fine.'

'Take these notes.' Mansi placed two thick registers in JD's hands. 'And thank you once again.'

JD's fingers touched Mansi's, sending shock waves through his body. Why do these girls want to electrocute you when they can kill with just one look? Mansi didn't retract her hand, and the 440 volts direct current kept on coursing through poor JD's numb body.

'Okay then, bye,' Mansi turned to leave.

'Take care,' JD mumbled.

'You too.'

JD returned to his room in a daze. Why was it that he always behaved like a bumbling idiot around Mansi? Why and for what was he so desperate? There were no simple answers to these complex questions and more importantly, this was hardly the time to search for them. The final exams were hanging like the sword of Damocles over his head.

Mehul was at his desk, mugging anatomy notes. 'I just can't remember the names of these bloody carpal bones of the wrist joint,' he cursed.

JD came out of his reverie. 'There is a simple mnemonic for them—*Suman Lata Tinde Paka, Tinde Tere Kachche Hain.*'

'Who is Suman Lata, your girlfriend?' Mehul joked.

'You fool, I'm trying to help you remember the names of the eight carpal bones in correct sequence. Just concentrate. *Suman: Scaphoid; Lata: Lunate; Tinde: Triquetral; Paka: Pisiform; Tinde: Trapezium; Tere: Trapezoid; Kachche: Capitate; Hain: Hamate.* The first four are in the proximal row and the other four are in the distal row. If you don't like tindas, there is another mnemonic for this—*She Looks Too Pretty Try To Catch Her.*' Spoken like a true FOSLA member.

'Thanks, I like tindas so I'll go with the first one.' Mehul jotted down the mnemonics alongside his notes.

A three-week preparatory break before the exams had begun. Night after night and all through the waking hours, the students toiled with just one aim, to do well in the exams. Some hoped to just pass the exams while some wanted to grab the top ranks.

The papers in the final exams were not that tough or maybe

they appeared easy because the students had put in a lot of hard work. They knew that if they prepared well, their confidence levels would be high, helping them to do well. The finals were over in a jiffy with most students more or less satisfied with their performance in conformity with the basic aim of the teachers, who set the papers in such a manner that an average student could solve 50 per cent of the questions.

There was a lot of excitement and bonhomie on the last day of the exams. Hostellers were especially excited as they were going home for a whole month. The students were, as yet, not even close to passing the MBBS exam, but that didn't matter to their families who already addressed them as 'doctors'.

Students like JD and Mansi, who had a real chance of topping in the first professional, did not reveal how they had fared in the viva voce. All they were ready to concede was that they had done well, but there was no stopping Junaid and Co. who were effusive in their self-praise. They told JD how they had bowled over Dr S. S. Das and Dr O. P. Mathur by their replies. JD listened to their bragging with patience and smiled encouragingly. He, too, wanted his dear friends to clear the exams so that they could continue their onward journey together.

7

It's Vacation Time

The one-month vacation began immediately after the exams. The top floor of the boys' hostel, inhabited mostly by juniors, wore a deserted look. Mehul and JD both were leaving at night, JD by the Tamil Nadu Express to New Delhi and Mehul by the Jhelum Express to Dhond, near Pune; their trains left Bhopla station within an hour or so of each other. Junaid, accompanied by Lazarus and Manish, provided the transport, driving JD and Mehul to the station in his father's Second World War vintage Willys Jeep. Such jeeps abounded in Bhopla and were popularly called 'Jugaads'. They were over-restored, brightly painted, open-top beauties in which Bhopla families loved to cruise around the town in the evenings.

'When are the results expected?' Manish asked no one in particular.

'I hope not for another thirty days. At least we'll be able to enjoy our holidays. Who knows what's in store for us?' Junaid responded with his earthy humour.

'I am sure we will all manage to pass, but this does not apply to JD,' Lazarus joined in the fun.

'What do you mean?' JD smiled knowingly.

'Because for you, passing is not an issue. It's a question of what rank you will get,' Lazarus shot back.

'Ammi has sent these for you,' Junaid took out two packages

of food from a plastic bag. JD and Mehul grabbed them and pushed them inside their luggage.

'My cousin works in the admininistrative office at Bhopla University. He will let us know the results the moment they are out,' Lazarus informed his friends on the way to the station.

'Have I given you my Delhi number or not? I'll change the SIM as soon as the train enters NCR,' JD told Lazarus.

'We all have it, for God's sake!' Junaid answered in Lazarus's wake. 'What about you, Mehul, will you also change your SIM?'

'I am not sure, but JD has my home landline number. He will inform me about my result,' Mehul answered.

Junaid parked his 'Jugaad' in a side alley just outside the station thereby saving a solid ten bucks. In honour of their departing friends, Manish and Lazarus manfully carried the luggage inside. Boys hate to spend their money on parking and porters, but for girls, they can empty their pockets faster than a flush tank.

JD's train was to arrive first followed by Mehul's. Instead of going to the waiting room, they decided to remain on the platform. There was the usual chaos intermingled with the stench of shit and smell of stale poori-bhaji. An urchin foolish enough to try his luck at begging was promptly shooed away by Junaid.

'Hey, two hot chicks have materialized on my radar,' Manish informed the others, stretching his body up to his full height.

'Where?' Lazarus's wide nostrils flared up even wider as if he was trying to smell them out.

'Abe gadhon, you donkeys, they are Mansi and Minal,' said Junaid.

'So what? They still qualify as hot chicks,' retorted Manish.

'What are they doing here?' asked Mehul.

'Surely they have not come to wish us bon voyage. They must also be going home,' said JD.

'Hiieee!' chorused Mansi and Minal on seeing the gang. They

were dressed in formal salwar kameezes, appropriate for long train journeys. An old coolie lugging their combined baggage chugged along with them. JD and Mehul were in badly creased jeans and faded T-shirts and although JD still managed to retain his cool-dude persona, Mehul was looking distinctly unkempt.

'Going home?' JD asked Minal, as Mansi was a step behind.

'Yes. I am going to Agra by the Tamil Nadu Express and Mansi to Pune by the Jhelum Express.'

'That means we both are on the same train while Mansi and Mehul will be together,' said JD wistfully. How he wished it was the other way round, but then you can't fight destiny. It was predestined that Mehul and Mansi would travel together on the Jhelum Express for the entire five years of their time in the medical college. It was destiny that made Mehul sit plumb in the middle of Mansi and Minal at the dissection table. Sorry boy, he thought ruefully, that's life!

'Why are you standing on the platform? There's still plenty of time—let's sit in the waiting room,' suggested Mansi.

'No, we are enjoying the crowds,' said Junaid foolishly, and immediately received dirty looks from the other boys.

'No problems, have fun. See you then.' The girls went off towards the waiting room. JD, Mehul, Manish and Lazarus were crestfallen.

'I would have kicked your ass hard if you had not come in your "Jugaad" to drop me to the station. This is the height of foolishness, man! The girls invited you to be with them and you actually refused. When will you learn?' JD was furious.

'Sorry, JD, I thought we were having a good time together. As it is we won't meet for a whole month.'

JD kept shaking his head in dismay. 'What a fool you are! You will never get a girl in your life.'

'Don't be ridiculous, JD,' Manish intervened. 'If you wish to, you can go sit with the girls in the waiting room. We will inform you when your train's arrival is announced.'

JD grabbed the opportunity. 'I think I'll do that. My legs are aching already.'

'To me it looks more like a case of an aching heart than aching legs.' Junaid clutched at his heart in a mock display of discomfort.

'Does anyone want to come with me?' JD asked as he strode away without looking back. He was a walking illustration of how girls can effortlessly make besotted males appear like utter fools and how girls have the power to break friendships and turn friends into foes.

'Hey, you two!' JD called out, trying to catch up with Minal and Mansi.

Mansi looked back, her face lighting up with pleasure. 'So, you have decided to abandon your friends,' she teased JD.

'It's a small sacrifice for your company, actually.'

'I am flattered.' Mansi fluttered her eyelashes tantalizingly.

JD held his breath momentarily. '*Kya katilana adaa hai*, what a killer style!' he muttered.

'Did you say something?'

JD wanted to say, 'You are looking very beautiful. You always look beautiful. Everything lights up when you are around. I am enamoured by you.' But all he said was, 'No, nothing, let's go and sit in the waiting room.'

The waiting room was overflowing with people of all shapes and sizes, some sleeping in asanas even Baba Ramdev would be proud of. Two or three mongrel dogs had managed to sneak in and were snugly ensconced in a corner under a large wooden table. A fat, middle-aged woman attendant wearing a blue pathani suit stopped Mansi and Minal as they tried to enter the waiting room. 'Houjful, medam. No place. Go sit outside.'

JD craned his neck and peeped inside. The waiting room was

indeed chock-a-block with passengers. 'Let's go back and join the gang,' he declared.

They trudged back to where the gang was standing on the platform. All JD's plans to sit with Mansi for a chat came to nought. He was planning to get her cell number, but now, with everyone around, it would be too great a risk. What if she refused? He didn't want a possible 'yes' to turn into a probable 'no' because of the presence of others.

'What happened? Why is Nawab sahib back on the platform among us?' Junaid resorted to leg-pulling.

'Don't try to act smart. We decided it would be nice to be together before we departed for the vacations.' JD's reply was as convincing as Casanova's claim to celibacy.

Shortly after, the Tamil Nadu Express arrived and JD and Minal boarded the third AC coach. They kept hovering around the door till the train left Bhopla station. The Jhelum Express was late as usual, so Junaid, Manish and Lazarus left after wishing Mehul and Mansi a safe journey.

The Jhelum Express finally arrived at 12 p.m. Mehul mused, 'For once the Indian Railways has named a train correctly. The Jhelum truly is a very jhilau train.' He boarded the three-tier sleeper coach while Mansi got into the second AC bogey. If JD had known they were not sitting next to each other, he would have had a more sound sleep on his upper berth in the Tamil Nadu Express.

⊕

Three weeks into the vacations, the results were out. Lazarus called up JD. On seeing his name flash on the screen, JD picked up the phone immediately. 'Hello.'

'Hi, JD. How's life?'

'*Total masti chal rahi hai*. I'm having fun. How are you all?'

'We are fine. The results are out—and guess what? You've got a distinction in anatomy.'

'But what's my overall rank?'

'You have come second. Sumit Saxena has topped with a distinction in biochemistry.'

'So he has done his father proud again.'

'You know how it is.'

'Yes I know, but still it rankles. Who's come third?'

'You won't be able to guess who it is.'

'Is it Mansi?'

'No. You won't be able to guess.'

'Tell me.'

'It's Bhavesh Mehta. Mansi is fourth.'

JD kept brooding long after the conversation. Although he was riled by the news, getting unduly upset was not his style. He was determined to defeat the forces that were trying to drag him back. He knew that an arrow can be shot only by dragging the bowstring back. So when life drags you back with unfavourable results, it is preparing to launch you to victory.

8
The Budding Docs

Clinical postings in medicine, surgery and obstetrics/gynaecology begin in the second professional of the MBBS course. This is the first time a medical student comes in contact with patients, and the feeling is truly heady. New aprons and shining stethoscopes make every student feel and behave like a real doctor. During this period, no medico is willing to remove his stetho from around his neck, even while sleeping!

JD and the gang arrived in the male medical ward at 9.30 sharp after attending the morning class. They, along with ten other students, had been posted there on a month-long rotation. None of them knew what exactly was expected of them so they just stood in the middle of the ward fiddling with their brand-new stethos.

JD was taken aback when he saw his batchmate Dhananjay Singh examining a male patient on bed number twenty-one. Dhananjay had obviously arrived early, by skipping the morning class. Two young nurses and several apron-clad students of the immediate senior batch had positioned themselves around him strategically. After a few minutes, Dhananjay proceeded to bed number twenty-two and studied the patient's treatment sheet. The group followed him and stood looking at him reverently.

Dhananjay was six feet tall and heavily built, with a nice little paunch. His large ruddy face and receding hairline made him look like a professor. The trainee nurses and the students had unwittingly mistaken him for a senior doctor and started to follow him, thinking he was taking morning rounds of the patients. Dhananjay, quite oblivious to the reason why he was getting so much attention, moved to bed number twenty-three and the group followed him blindly.

This herd mentality is not unique to the medical profession, but still, it is more commonly seen in medical colleges than in other educational institutions. Since medicine is mostly a hands-on science, learning skills like examining patients is of paramount importance. These skills can only be learnt from the teachers in the bedside clinics. In other professions, books can be a substitute for a teacher but in medicine no book can ever replace a teacher. Only an experienced teacher can teach a medical student how to examine a patient correctly.

JD was quick to decipher the unfolding comedy of errors. He quietly went up to Dhananjay and winked. 'What is this patient suffering from, sir?'

Dhananjay was a smart bloke, so he immediately got the hint that he had been confused for a senior consultant. He first looked intently at the swollen feet and then at the bulging abdomen of the patient and remarked, 'Well, this is a serious disease. As you all can see, the patient is quite ill. His entire body is bloated up. Let's not disturb him right now. I'll tell you about his condition in detail later.'

'All the students of the new batch, please come to the seminar room,' commanded Dr Deepak Bhargav, senior resident of the department of medicine, emerging from the duty room. Dhananjay was the first to rush to the safety of the seminar room, avoiding the murderous looks thrown at him by the students of the senior batch.

⊕

A medical student is not supposed to enter the anatomy dissection hall without *Cunningham's Manual*. Similarly, before entering the medicine ward, the student must have *Hutchison's Clinical Methods* on his person. Students caught without them are doomed. The initial clinical posting is almost entirely devoted to learning how to take the proper history of a patient and conducting a basic medical examination. Senior residents and consultants teach students to take down the main complaints of the patient in chronological order, to ask a detailed history of past illnesses and to note down the relevant family history. The importance of sound, accurate history-taking cannot be overemphasized. It greatly helps to ensure that the examination and investigation proceed in the right direction and provide important clues to a correct diagnosis.

Every day, a case was allotted to students for history-taking and examination. Any of the students could be randomly asked to present the case later, which encouraged the full involvement of all the students. One morning, the students were asked to examine a sixty-year-old male patient suffering from chronic asthma.

'What's your name?' asked JD, taking the lead.

'With what complaints were you admitted to the hospital?' asked Mansi, butting in.

The patient was an old hand at these matters. He had been admitted to the male medical ward several times in the past due to frequent attacks of asthma. The moment he saw fresh-faced medical students approach him, he feigned sleep.

'What's your name, Baba?' JD repeated with the utmost politeness. The patient didn't respond. JD looked up helplessly and shrugged his shoulders. 'How are we going to complete the history-taking and examination of the patient?'

'What are you suffering from, Baba?' Mansi asked again in the sweetest possible manner.

'Can you give me a bundle of Sher Chhaap Bidi?' asked Baba, opening his eyes.

'But you aren't supposed to smoke, you are ill,' rebuked Mansi.

'If you are so worried about my health, give me fifty rupees so that I can eat apples. The hospital food is making me sick.'

'If you promise to cooperate, we will give you twenty rupees,' JD tried to bargain.

'Make it thirty and you have a deal.'

The deal was struck and Baba told them his own history, and his family's, in minute detail, some of it true, most of it fabricated. He was quite an expert at it, having told and retold his story to several budding docs over and over again. Junaid was almost certain that he had all the symptoms of asthma. During the posting Junaid had been convinced that he was suffering from such diseases as tuberculosis, rheumatic heart, stones in the kidney, cancer of the throat, and cirrhosis of liver, all of which successfully cleared up in a few days. This is a common phenomenon seen in budding doctors who develop a morbid fascination for various diseases.

⊕

The next rotation landed JD's batch in the department of surgery. Dr Parshu Ram Tripathi, HOD of surgery, was a terror not only among students but also patients. True to his initials, Dr P. R. Tripathi was passionate about teaching per rectal (PR) examination to the students since he believed this was an important part of their curriculum.

PR is usually done to diagnose prostate enlargement in elderly male patients. Once admitted to the surgical ward, the patient became Dr P. R. Tripathi's sole focus and obsession. Any elderly patient with difficulty in passing urine is usually suspected of having a prostate enlargement, also called BPH (Benign Prostate

Hyperplasia). If the enlargement was significant and the patient developed urinary retention, he had to be operated upon immediately. Those with a minor enlargement and mild difficulty in passing urine had to wait for their turn. As Dr P. R. Tripathi's OT list was usually long, this period could vary from a fortnight to a month. Ganpat Rai was one such patient and was waiting for his turn for close to a month. In the meantime his enlarged prostate was being used to teach clinical skills to the budding doctors. JD and his batchmates saw the examiner putting on a rubber glove and applying a lubricant like Vaseline on the index finger to push it into the patient's anal opening to feel for the enlarged prostate gland. During his morning rounds, Dr P. R. Tripathi liked to be followed by a crowd of residents, housemen, nurses and medical students. After breezing through the first five or six patients with non-prostatic problems he stopped beside Ganpat Rai's bed and made notes on his folder, all set to perform the surgery. The doctor was an expert on the prostate gland and it was rumoured that he was close to touching the magical figure of one thousand prostatectomy operations. That one day he may get listed in *The Guinness Book of World Records* as the top prostate surgeon in the world, was the rumour on the college campus.

9
Digitalization

Pharmacology, pathology, microbiology and forensic medicine are the four main subjects taught in the second professional. Dr S. K. Patil, an associate professor, was probably the best teacher of pharmacology in the medical college. There was usually full attendance and pin-drop silence in his class. Dr Patil had started a series of lectures on cardiac drugs. He was teaching the students about an important cardiac drug, Digitalis, and everybody was concentrating hard. Digitalis, popularly known as digoxin, is an all-time favourite of examiners. If a question isn't included in the theory paper, it's sure to figure in the viva voce.

'Digitalis increases the force of contraction of the heart. It also has the property to control tachycardia, that is, it reduces the rapidity of the heart rate. Thus it is the most commonly used drug in heart failure.' Dr Patil paused before continuing, 'The process of administering Digitalis to the patient is known as digitalization. It is split into rapid and slow digitalization, depending upon the need of the patient.' At the end of his lecture, Dr Patil reminded everyone of the impending class test on Saturday.

JD closed his notebook and leaned back in his seat. He had been planning to take Mansi out for a movie for quite some time. Each time he approached her, he developed tachycardia (rapid heart rate). The question could not come out as his heart was in his mouth, blocking the outflow of words. He considered popping in a Digitalis tablet before popping out the all-important question. A wry smile appeared on his face.

'Why are you smiling? Did you like Dr Patil's lecture so much that you are feeling blessed?' Mansi stopped in the aisle near JD's seat.

'I don't know how good Dr Patil's lecture was, but I am sure about Digitalis being a damn good drug for certain boys who develop tachycardia when they are around certain girls.'

Mansi laughed out loud. 'Are you trying to tell me something?'

Her encouraging laugh almost killed JD. 'Yes, I want you to know that you have that effect on me.'

Mansi blushed and JD almost died again. 'I was thinking of asking you out for a movie,' he somehow managed to say.

'But we have a class test in microbiology this Wednesday and then Dr Patil is taking a test on Saturday.'

'That's true.' JD's voice showed his disappointment.

'By the way, which movie did you plan to see?'

'*Guzarish*.'

'Even I wanted to watch it. Hrithik is my favourite actor and the topic of euthanasia interests me. Can't we go on Sunday?'

'It may not run so long. Critics have liked it so it's going to be a sure-shot flop.'

'Then let's catch the evening show, the class tests can wait. But Minal will kill me if I went alone.'

JD's accelerating heart beat went down without Digitalis. The wave of excitement that had swept his body abated suddenly. The prospect of Minal being there with Mansi in the darkened hall somehow didn't appear appealing at all. 'Okay, I'll also ask Mehul to come along. He keeps copying Hrithik's dance steps so he'd love to see the movie.'

'Then it's done. I'll meet you at Fun Cinemas for the 6 p.m. show.' Mansi went down the aisle and out of the lecture theatre.

JD kept sitting in his seat, a bit confused. He didn't know whether to feel happy or sad. Mansi had accepted his invitation but with a rider. He thought how life is full of such little complications, and the sooner one realizes that nothing is simple, the better it is for one.

JD and Mehul arrived at Fun Cinemas around 5.45 and stood near the booking window to wait for Mansi and Minal. They had checked their monetary position before coming and the balance sheet didn't look very healthy. The total expendable amount was in the vicinity of ₹900, which meant that they needed to be very careful about how they used it.

'The tickets would cost ₹680, which leaves us with only 220 bucks to treat them,' Mehul presented the budget for the evening entertainment.

'We have to get popcorn and Pepsi in the interval, otherwise it will look cheap,' commented JD.

'Even if we share two tubs of popcorn with small colas it will cost ₹360. We don't have that much to spare.'

'Come, let's check out the ice cream parlour—they usually have some cheap offers,' JD got up and walked towards the parlour. 'Hey look, the cassata slice is for thirty bucks only.'

Mehul came up behind JD and checked the price list. Left to him he would have gone for the orange bar, but he knew JD wouldn't agree to that. 'That's it then, cassata slice it is. We will still be left with some cash after treating them.'

'I think we can take the girls to McD for a McPuff after the movie. It won't cost much and we will be able to spend some more time with them,' suggested JD with an expansive sweep of his hands.

'Let's not overdo it, a movie and ice cream are enough,' Mehul's middle-class mentality came to the fore.

'What are you two discussing so seriously, the micro or the

pharmac test?' Mansi had come up the escalator and was standing just behind them.

JD and Mehul almost jumped out of their pants. Mehul looked at Mansi nervously. Had she heard his last comment? There was no way to know that. 'Where is Minal?' he asked.

'She wasn't feeling well so she dropped out.' Mansi's reply was as convincing as a politician's promise to fight corruption.

Mehul's spirits dipped but JD perked up. The budgetary constraints were no more applicable. Breathing easy, JD went to the booking window to purchase the tickets.

'Come, let's go inside, the movie should be starting any minute now,' he shouted, flashing the tickets towards Mansi and Mehul.

A bored-looking usher was leaning against the door. He tore off their tickets with a barely concealed yawn and returned the remaining halves. JD led the way and guided Mansi to seat number B1, he himself occupied B2 and Mehul understandingly settled down in B3. The hall was pretty much empty; it seemed no one was interested in euthanasia.

'Would you like to have something to eat or drink?' asked JD.

'No, thank you. I had tea just before leaving the hostel.'

'A Pepsi perhaps,' JD insisted.

'Why are you forcing her to have a cold drink after hot tea? Mixing thanda-garam is bad for the throat, it will harm her singing voice.' Mehul pinched JD hard to indicate that there was no need to splurge unnecessarily.

'Okay, yaar!' JD hissed in Mehul's ear.

The hall lights dimmed and the advertisements of paan masalas started. Watching all these ads one would believe that the staple diet of Indians was paan masalas and gutkhas and not proteins and carbohydrates. People gradually trickled in, holding popcorn tubs and cold drinks. A young couple walked in hand-in-hand and went straight towards the extreme corner seats at the back of the hall.

'Hey, they seem to be Simran Saxena and Tarun Gupta,' Mehul whispered. Mansi and JD looked in their direction but didn't comment. Simran and Tarun were in the junior final year and had been going steady since their first professional days. Their relationship was considered an antithesis to the concept of FOSLA as both appeared to be equally devoted to each other. Tarun Gupta was the son of Dean Dr S. K. Gupta, while Simran was the daughter of a local businessman.

Shortly afterwards, the film started and the trio became engrossed in the true-to-life depiction of Hrithik as a quadriplegic (a person with paralysis of all four limbs). After some time they were distracted by the activities in the seats occupied by Simran and Tarun who appeared to be all over each other.

'I think if they carry on like this people will soon have their backs to the screen,' commented Mehul.

'Oh, come on, they are compensating for the lack of onscreen action,' JD remarked snidely.

'Shut up, you cheapos. You are behaving worse than the street majnus,' Mansi admonished them.

'Tell this to your Simran didi and Tarun jijaji. If we are being cheap then they are also not setting a gold standard for dignified behaviour,' Mehul became agitated. His middle-class values were deeply entrenched and this open display of passion in public had unnerved him.

'Cool it, guys. Let's enjoy the film.' JD tried to pacify Mansi and Mehul.

In the interval, according to their plan, Mehul went out to buy cassata slices. JD had requested Mehul to leave him and Mansi alone for a few moments so that he could whisper some sweet-nothings in her ears. But the cootchie-cooing happening in the back seat held him back. It would have looked frivolous and demeaning if he had expressed his feelings for Mansi at that moment. When the film restarted, Tarun and Simran left the scene in the cover of darkness, probably they had seen their juniors during the interval and didn't want any gossip to spread the next day.

The next day, there was a full question on the effects and side effects of Digitalis in the pharmacology class test. The evening spent watching the film had taken its toll. All three—JD, Mansi and Mehul—got digitalized, that is, their hearts sank and they developed bradycardia (slow heart rate) on seeing the paper because they had not mugged Digitalis well.

10
What a Cricket Match!

The second professional of the MBBS course spans one year and a half with a single exam at the end. The students remain in a state of suspended animation during the initial part with studies being the last thing on their agenda. Some busy themselves with 'bird'watching (especially migratory birds in tight jeans and tighter tops), while some others are involved in watching movies and still others turn to sports.

The intercollegiate cricket tournament was on and JD, Lazarus and Bhavesh Mehta were in the Nehru Medical College team as the opening batsman, wicketkeeper and medium pacer respectively. They had defeated the Rajiv Gandhi College of Commerce in the first round and were now up against a tough opponent in the Indira Gandhi College of Technology (IGCT). Having defeated the college named after the grandson, would NMC, which bore the name of the grandfather be able to defeat the college christened after the daughter? What the hell? How does it matter if the grandfather defeats the grandson and then wins or loses against the daughter? Whew! Sounds like a nice little riddle, showing that Indians thrive on flattery. After all, no one told us to name all our institutions after the trinity, certainly not Nehruji.

Although an official holiday had not been declared, most of the boys and a substantial number of NMC girls had absconded from classes and were present at the ground to witness the match.

As far as IGCT was concerned, every single student with the Y chromosome had reached the venue. Obviously, they were not great patrons of the game of cricket; they had come to ogle at the plentiful medico girls. IGCT, for that matter, most engineering colleges including the IITs, are an impoverished lot where girls are concerned. They have an eternal shortage of the X chromosome in their institutions and have to make do with the available resources, which may or not be much in quality or quantity.

The IGCT team won the toss and elected to bat. The NMC bowling attack was spearheaded by the fearsome pace duo of Aashish Paul and Shirish Kamboj. Aashish drew first blood and soon Shirish removed the other opener. IGCT lost half the side before the score reached 50, but the lower-order batsmen hit some lusty blows and they reached 100 in the nineteenth over. There was a lot of cheering by the IGCT boys whenever a boundary was struck. The NMC students vigorously booed at the fall of each wicket. There were some heated exchanges and tempers ran high. Both Aashish and Shirish had finished their quota so Bhavesh bowled the last over. It turned out to be a nightmare for NMC as he gave away 24 runs and the IGCT team finished at 124 for 8 wickets from its 20 overs.

After a break of fifteen minutes, JD and Rajan Dave arrived in the ground to open the NMC innings. IGCT also had a tear-away fast bowler in Bhuvnesh Agrawal, nicknamed Bachchu. He had shining, white teeth adorning a jutting upper jaw, which gave him a permanently snarling look. No one knew in which semester he was, whether he had cleared his final semester or was still a student of IGCT, but surely he had been in the college for a long, long time. Of course not as long as Riyaaz Mamu, who was in a different league altogether.

Rajan Dave took a single off the very first ball bowled by Bachchu, which brought JD to the batting crease. Bachchu went back to the start of his fairly long run up. He started to run in slowly, gathered speed and leapt up in the air before delivering a short-pitched bouncer. JD swayed back as the ball zipped past his nose.

'Buck-up, Bachchu. Buck-up!' The crowd roared in murderous frenzy.

Bachchu motored in again and bowled an out-swinger. JD slashed at it and the ball flew past the third slip to the boundary.

'JayDee, JayDee.' The girls started to shout in perfect unison. A cacophony of cheering came from the boys.

Bachchu didn't allow JD to score any further runs in his over and the crowd's excitement gradually died down. Rajan Dave and JD settled down and started to score freely. The total mounted up rapidly to 50 for no loss in 7 overs. The IGCT captain changed tactics and deployed Aamod Jha, a leg spinner from the pavilion end. The first ball slipped out of his hand and bounced three or four times before reaching Rajan Dave. Rajan jumped out of his crease in sheer glee and tried to lift the ball over the bowler's head but it went below the bat and crashed into the stumps. This triggered a mini collapse and NMC lost 4 more wickets in quick succession for the addition of only 10 runs.

Lazarus walked in at the loss of the fifth wicket. JD was still there and they stitched together a crucial 30-run partnership. Lazarus was given out leg-before-wicket to an incoming delivery bowled by Bachchu. Lazarus stood at the crease in protest as he felt the ball going down the leg. There was a heated exchange between Bachchu and Lazarus before the umpires intervened and Lazarus reluctantly left the field.

Six NMC wickets were down at the score of 90, and 35 runs still remained to be scored in the remaining 5 overs. Two more wickets fell with the addition of only 20 runs. The ninth wicket was run out at the score of 118 on the fourth ball of the nineteenth over. In walked Bhavesh Mehta, the last man. He fended off the last 2 balls of the penultimate over successfully. The only hope now was JD who was still there with 44 runs to his credit.

NMC needed 7 runs to win off the last over being bowled by Bachchu with JD on strike. JD played the first ball to deep fine leg and could have easily taken a single but desisted because he didn't want to expose Bhavesh to the pace of Bachchu. Of the next ball JD collected 2 runs in the midwicket area and moved on to 46. Now 5 runs were needed off 4 balls.

Bachchu next bowled a well-directed yorker, which JD just about managed to dig out—5 *off 3 balls*.

Bachchu came charging in again and sent down a short-pitched bouncer, which sailed over JD's head—5 *off 2 balls*.

The IGCT crowd stood up on its feet and started to cheer Bachchu loudly. JD drove the next ball with tremendous power and it raced away to the long off boundary for 4 runs. The scores were now tied at 124. One ball left and one run needed. JD's half-century was celebrated with a loud '*Bholay ke bhai bum*'. Several girls jumped up and did an impromptu jig. The IGCT boys attempted a few cheap remarks but their yells were drowned in the loud roar of the medicos.

The IGCT captain and wicketkeeper rushed towards Bachchu and they had a long mid-pitch conference. Bachchu walked back slowly to the top of his bowling mark. The entire crowd went silent. No cheering, no hooting, just a suspense-filled silence. Bachchu ran in firing on all cylinders, leapt up and bowled an in-swinging delivery, which eluded JD's bat and crashed into the stumps. One half of the crowd was shell-shocked, the other half erupted in ecstasy. The IGCT team started hugging and congratulating each other for having eked out a win by the skin of their teeth. According to the rules, if a match ended in a tie, the team that had lost fewer wickets was declared the winner. IGCT had lost only 8 wickets while NMC had lost all 10.

After a moment, JD and Bhavesh started to jump up and down the pitch with glee, signalling the V sign towards the stands. The umpire had declared a no-ball, which meant JD was not out and at the same time, one run was added to the NMC score. There was no need to bowl the no-ball again as NMC's score was already 125—one more than IGCT's.

The medicos went berserk with delight. Dancing led by the girls erupted in the stands occupied by the NMC crowd. This irked the IGCT boys and they started to throw not only abuse but also all sorts of missiles, whatever they could lay their hands on. The medicos retaliated with choicest abuses, grotesque gestures and determined stone-throwing. In the midst of this all-out war, Mansi and the girls rushed and hugged JD who lost his balance and fell down. Several maidens toppled over him as he lay on the maidan. Loud sighs escaped from the mouths of boys on both sides, NMC as well as IGCT.

Twenty-odd NMC students received minor cuts and bruises and were taken in the college bus to the hospital emergency for treatment. A few stupid IGCT students also arrived in the emergency section for first-aid and were treated with slaps and kicks, forcing them to run away to save their lives.

11
Aftermath of the Match

The girls' hostel was full of chatter that night. It ranged from praise to criticism about Mansi and her gang's shameless behaviour. Their hugging and falling all over JD in full public view invited admiration, jealousy as well as censure.

Meanwhile, the undergraduate boys' hostel reverberated with the heady air of victorious celebration.

A grand drink party was organized by the Gestapo in the PG hostel to celebrate the cricket team's victory. The entire team along with Riyaaz Mamu, the unofficial coach, had been invited. As usual Maheen Bhai was looking after the catering, and Rajeev Gaur and Manmohan (Mannu) Sharma, senior Gestapo members, were supervising the 'drunk' arrangements. It would be wrong to use the word 'drink' because the whole emphasis was on getting totally sloshed. In fact the 'drunk' arrangements were pretty straightforward. Pour two full bottles of Old Monk into a large steel bucket, add two litres of Coke and drop large chunks of ice in it. Stir well and the rum cola was ready. It's another story that halfway through the party the daaru was always over and some junior Gestapo member had to go all the way to the nearby Shivhare Wines to fetch fresh stock.

By 9 p.m., the Gestapo Headquarters located in room 111 was throbbing with excitement. The aroma of human sweat enriched with tobacco smoke and laced with ganja created a strong hypnotic effect. A naked bulb hanging from the ceiling made the setting appear more sinister than it actually was. Tubelights had been purposefully switched off to create the necessary mood. Room 111 was in fact a large hall with an attached bathroom and a small kitchenette meant for the assistant warden. As the assistant warden was almost always a Gestapo member, the room had become its HQ by default. No one had the guts to challenge this arrangement because the price would have been too heavy to pay.

The large steel bucket atop the lone table was full to its brim with rum cola. A variety of glasses in all shapes and sizes stood by its side along with stacks of salted groundnuts, chips, kurkure and fresh salad. Maheen Bhai entered the room and handed over a battered and bruised steel jug to Mannu Sharma. The jug, a witness to hundreds of parties and brawls in room 111, had historical value and thus could not be discarded. Similarly Maheen Bhai, a teetotaler, was always in the thick of things during these wild sessions.

Mannu dipped the jug in the bucket and filled up the glasses with rum cola. Rajeev Gaur, assistant warden and the present occupant of the room, passed them on. When everyone had a glass in his hand, Rajeev and Mannu raised the NMC chant 'Bholay ke bhai bum...' Everyone joined in as glasses were raised to lips and drained in ten seconds flat. The second round was more subdued as people decided to breathe and talk in between large swigs of rum cola.

JD had acquired instant celebrity status after his scintillating performance in the match. Together with his good academic record, he was sure to become an associate Gestapo member. Everyone wanted him to take a sip from his glass, the ultimate way of showing true camaraderie and chumminess.

Most stood up and started to sway to a raunchy Bollywood number in a drunken stupor. JD was pushed to the centre and given a chance to display his dancing skills. JD obliged by copying Akshay Kumar in the film *Action Replay*. Mannu and Rajeev jumped into the fray and thrust their pelvis provocatively, trying to imitate Aishwarya Rai.

The dancing picked up speed with most dancers twisting, turning, writhing, undulating, shaking and vibrating in their very own, inimitable style. Maybe here was a chance for Saroj Khan and other Mumbai choreographers to pick up a step or two. The basic funda was to flay your limbs, jerk your head and twist your torso to its maximum tensile strength, all the while maintaining a full-toothed smile fixed on your face with your eyes totally glazed out.

The vigorous jumping and shaking caused the rum cola to mix thoroughly with the gastric juices, especially the hydrochloric acid. This set in motion a strong chemical reaction resulting in the production of profuse fumes which came out of the mouth in the form of an overpowering stench. The few non-drinkers inhaling these fumes achieved instant nirvana.

The drinking and dancing reached a crescendo and soon enough, the bucket of rum cola was empty. As was the tradition, Shantanu Sikarwar, a junior Gestapo member, was asked to go to Shivhare Wines to fetch more Old Monk. Shantanu went downstairs and took out his Pulsar bike from the basement parking. He opened the tank and tried to assess the quantity of petrol in the light of his mobile. No one dared to leave more than half a litre of petrol in the tank otherwise it was sure to be stolen. There was very little petrol in the tank but enough for a to-and-fro trip to Shivhare Wines.

There was a large congregation of drunken IGCT boys at the wine shop. Most were armed with rods and chains and some even carried sharp weapons. No one took any notice of Shantanu as he stood quietly and listened.

'It's almost midnight, let's go and screw the bastards,' a tall, gangly boy with unruly hair suggested.

'Let's wait for some more time. Most of the bastards in the medical hostel remain awake, mugging late into the night,' a short, stocky guy remarked.

A few tough-looking boys joined the discussion to decide the best time for attacking the UG (undergraduate) hostel of Nehru Medical College. Shantanu sneaked away quickly and sped like hell on his bike to reach the PG hostel in five minutes flat.

'They are planning to attack the UG hostel!' blurted Shantanu, bursting into the Gestapo den. He was trembling with excitement and his breath came out in sharp, short gasps.

'Calm down! Who is planning to attack the UG hostel?' Riyaaz Mamu stood up to his full six-feet-two-inches height.

'There is a group of around thirty to forty IGCT boys gathered at Shivhare Wines. They are armed with iron rods, chains and sticks. I heard them planning an attack on the UG hostel tonight.' Shantanu wiped the sweat from his forehead with the sleeve of his shirt.

'Let's gather everyone together and go bash the bastards,' Mannu shouted in a highly strung voice.

'No! That's not the way to do it. In an open fight, a lot of us can get seriously injured. Let them attack, we will take them by surprise.' Riyaaz Mamu was a veteran of several intercollegiate wars and his expertise in such matters was indisputable.

'What should we do?' Rajeev came up to Riyaaz Mamu.

'Call your friends in the UG hostel immediately and tell them about the attack being planned by the IGCT boys. Ask them to collect in the common hall and not to panic. Assure them that we are on our way with a foolproof plan to repel any such attack.' Riyaaz Mamu's voice grew stern and his demeanour became officer-like. Long back, he had tried in vain to get into the National Defence Academy, Khadakwasla, Pune, but couldn't clear the entrance exam. The Indian Army's loss turned out to be Nehru Medical College's gain.

Riyaaz Mamu deputed Mannu and Rajeev to go to the UG hostel rightaway. 'Call everyone and collect as many stones as you can, then carry them to the rooftop quickly. There are a lot of waste motorcycle tyres lying in the basement so take them upstairs along with a bottle of petrol. Lock the channel gate properly and double secure it with a chain and lock.'

'You want us to throw burning tyres on the attackers?' Mannu's eyes lit up with perverse pleasure.

'That's the general idea.'

'What an idea, sirji!' Rajeev laughed out loud and everyone joined in.

'Select boys with strong arms who can aim accurately. The stones must hit the target, the burning tyres are to create panic,' Riyaaz Mamu instructed brusquely.

As the others were making the phone calls, Mannu and Rajeev took off on their bike for the UG hostel, which was located on the west side of the campus behind the new OPD blocks.

'What's the exact plan?' Shantanu asked Riyaaz Mamu.

'Well, first we'll have to collect the weapons from the Gol Bazaar area where some of my friends live. Basically iron rods, chains and hockey sticks, but I'll also try to get hold of a desi katta. You never know, sometimes things can get out of control and you need a real weapon to restore order.'

'I hope things don't reach that stage,' said Shantanu with apprehension.

'I am not expecting such a scenario, but it's better to take all precautions possible. Anyway, after picking up the weapons, we'll come back and hide near the OPD block. When attacked, the UG hostel boys will retaliate by throwing stones and burning tyres. This will create fear and confusion and we will take the IGCT boys from behind,' said Riyaaz Mamu, laying bare his battle plan.

Around 1.30 a.m., the attackers arrived on their bikes, which they parked just outside the campus gate. It was a dark, unusually humid night with a half moon lurking behind thick, woolly clouds. There was an eerie silence, not unlike the quiet before the storm. The attackers sneaked in under the cover of darkness and proceeded stealthily towards the UG hostel. They appeared to know the topography well.

The front gate of the UG hostel was chained and locked and most of the lights were switched off. The hostellers had collected a huge stockpile of stones on the rooftop along with some old tyres to be set on fire and thrown on the enemy. Riyaaz Mamu and his group were hiding in the OPD block, ready to take on the attackers when they retreated. The trap was laid and the victims were awaited.

The attack came in the form of a hail of stones, which broke several windowpanes of the hostel facade. The stone-throwing continued unabated and a few studious types got hit with flying glass and stones because their room lights were still on and it was easier to target them. The stone-pelting was merely a ploy to provide cover to their comrades who were going to attack the hostel gate any moment. The counterattack as envisaged by Riyaaz Mamu had to be kept on hold because the attackers were throwing stones from quite a distance.

After a few minutes amidst a loud war cry, a large group of IGCT boys attacked the hostel gate with rods and crowbars. They wanted to gain entry in the hostel and bash up the NMC boys so that in future they would not dare to take panga with them. The NMC boys atop the roof started to throw stones at the IGCT boys with great ferocity. Some hit their target, some missed, but they succeeded in making the attackers run for cover.

'Where is the bottle of petrol?' shouted Danav Sisodia.

'Right here,' Bhavesh Mehta raised the petrol bottle in his hand and started to sprinkle petrol on the tyres.

'Here goes!' screamed Danav, igniting and throwing a match on the wet tyres. They went up in a huge ball of fire that illuminated the entire roof.

'Give me an iron rod.' Danav appeared possessed as he lifted a burning tyre with the help of the rod and ran towards the parapet. Everyone looked in awe as he hurled the tyre down. The tyre landed near the hostel gate, barely missing the bunch of boys trying to break the lock on the gate. A few burning splinters fell on the clothes of the boys standing nearby—they shrieked in fear and backed off.

Within seconds, two more burning tyres thrown by Bhavesh and Mehul landed on the ground near the IGCT boys. As they retreated, they were caught in a volley of stones being thrown from the rooftop. Two or three boys got hit on the head and started to bleed profusely. There was panic in their ranks and they turned back and ran for dear life, leaving behind the rods and chains.

'*Bholay ke bhai bum, Bholay ke bhai bum, Bholay ke bhai bum, Bum Bholaay. Hari har, Hari har, Hari har...*' the NMC chant rang from the rooftop.

Near the OPD block, another reception party led by Riyaaz Mamu waited in the darkness. They chased the escaping IGCT boys and beat them up nice and proper. Shoes, sandals, slippers, torn T-shirts and a lonely helmet were left behind, serving as a grim reminder of the IGCT boys' misadventure.

The hostellers had come out and were huddled in small groups, talking animatedly. Riyaaz Mamu arrived at the scene of victory for NMC, their very own 'Haldighati Ka Maidan', and surveyed the scene nonchalantly. On seeing him they rushed forward and lifted him up in the air. Loud cheering rocked the night, 'Three cheers for Brigadier Mamu hip, hip, hurray…hip, hip, hurray…hip, hip, hurray!'

'It's everyone's victory, we all deserve the credit for it,' Riyaaz Mamu spoke modestly. Then he smiled impishly, 'But let's remove the tyres and stones. We don't want to get into trouble with the authorities.'

The debris was removed in a jiffy and the tired warriors went back inside the hostel after carefully relocking the gate. The seniors from the PG hostel had decided to spend the night with the UG boys as a precautionary measure against a second misadventure by the IGCT boys. But nothing happened and they all slept peacefully till late afternoon. Indeed they deserved the rest, every bit of it.

12
How Not to Deliver a Baby

Soon the excitement died down and the fight was all but forgotten as the daily grind of lectures, clinics and tests gathered momentum. JD's group had completed its surgical rotation and was now posted in the obstetrics and gynaecology (ObG) wards. All the boys in the group felt extremely ill at ease in the wards full of women with either protuberant bellies or with small, incessantly crying babies by their sides. The senior nurses treated the boys as unwelcome invaders and social outcasts. The elderly female 'attenders', mostly wizened, hawkish mother-in-laws, eyed them as potential rapists and baby snatchers. (It's really quite befuddling why attendants are called 'attenders' in Indian hospitals. Probably the same logic that makes Indians pack things in cartoons rather than cartons.)

Dr Veena Rao, a senior resident doing her postgraduation in the ObG department, was assigned to the students for clinical teaching in the wards. She was a thin, frail-looking female with a whiplash voice and curt manner—two essential traits of a successful gynaecologist. If you can't screech and shout like Dolly Bindra, the aggressive participant in *Big Boss*, the TV show, no woman will bear down during labour pains and no babies will come out of the womb.

'Today I'll tell you how to take the history of a patient in a pregnancy case,' Dr Veena Rao started her sermon in a loud, shrill voice, without resorting to any niceties or formalities of introduction. The ObG residents are always too tired and seldom exhibit any civic behaviour, which is understandable, since no one can after thirty-six hours of non-stop duty.

'First ask whether the patient is a primipara or a multipara. Try to ascertain accurately the LMP (last menstrual period) on which the calculation of the EDD (expected date of delivery) depends. In the case of a multipara always note down the parity, which includes both the live children she has delivered and the stillbirths. Specifically ask if there was any bleeding during the pregnancy period. You must also enquire about any leaking. Do not forget to ask about abortions. All this signifies a bad obstetric history. In such women we have to be extra cautious.' She went on and on making the boys' eyes glaze over with boredom.

After finishing her discourse, Dr Veena Rao went to a nearby bed occupied by a pale, pregnant woman. She produced a funnel-like instrument made of aluminum from her apron pocket. There were two collared openings at the two ends of the instrument, one small the other large. She placed the end with the larger opening on the patient's abdomen and listened carefully through the smaller opening. She kept moving the funnel over the patient's abdomen, all the while listening intently. Finally, she lifted the instrument and marked a cross with her ballpoint pen on the patient's abdomen.

Straightening up, she asked, 'Does anyone know what this instrument is called?' She was met with a stony silence, broken intermittently by shrieks emanating from the nearby labour room.

'This is a foetoscope,' she told the students, after waiting for few seconds. 'It is used to listen to foetal heart sounds. Can you tell me, what's the normal foetal heart rate?'

'It is 120 beats per minute,' JD replied.

'Good. Now put the foetoscope over the cross marked by me on the patient's abdomen and tell me the foetal heart rate.' Dr Veena Rao handed JD the foetoscope.

JD approached the bulging abdomen hesitantly and applied the narrow end over the cross.

'Wrong!' Dr Veena Rao jumped forward and snatched the foetoscope from JD's hand. 'Always put the broader end on the abdomen and the narrow end near your ear,' she demonstrated to the students. 'Now do it correctly,' she commanded JD.

JD put the broader end of the foetoscope on the patient's abdomen and pressed his left ear to the narrow end. All he could hear was his pulse pounding at his temple. Through his right ear entered the sporadic shrieks coming from the labour room, intermingled with the loud sniggers of his batchmates. He was totally confused. All the time he kept looking at his wristwatch intently. The more he tried to concentrate, the more clear was the sound of his own pulse beating at his temple.

'Come on, tell me the foetal heart rate,' Dr Rao asked JD.

'It is 72 beats per minute.'

'What! I didn't ask for your heart rate. If the foetal heart rate is only 72, the foetus is in danger. This condition is called foetal bradycardia and is generally due to compromised oxygen supply to the foetus. Many of these cases are due to a tight loop of umbilical cord around the neck of the foetus. Now let me check for myself.' Dr Rao took the foetoscope from JD and listened carefully, looking at her wristwatch.

'The foetal heart rate is around 120 beats per minute,' she declared, looking pointedly at JD. 'So, there is no foetal bradycardia and no need to go in for an emergency caesarean section.'

Everyone smiled with relief as if they were the ones going to be asked to cut open the woman's abdomen to take out the baby. One by one they tried to listen to the foetal heart using the foetoscope. Most didn't hear anything, some heard the sounds of bowel movements and still others were happy to listen to gases moving around the abdomen. But they all agreed that the foetus was hale and hearty, kicking around merrily in the amniotic fluid, its heart going at a steady 120 beats per minute.

Dr Rao then asked the students to take the medical history of the patient in detail and vanished inside the labour room. The moment she turned her back, all the boys vanished from the stuffy, smelly, stifling atmosphere of the ObG ward. The girls remained inside, taking down the obstetric history of the patient diligently.

JD, Junaid, Lazarus, Manish and Mehul went to the college canteen and sat down at a table near the window giving a grand view of the non-functioning incinerator with heaps of medical and non-medical waste piled around it. Maheen Bhai was nowhere to be seen. On seeing JD and his gang, his assistant Sajju Phukki immediately brought five cups of tea to their table.

'Do you want something to eat with tea?' JD asked no one in particular.

'Yes, samosas would be just fine. The morning clinic has drained me mentally, physically and nutritionally,' lamented Lazarus. Everyone settled for samosas and tea.

⊕

The pathology class was due in fifteen minutes' time. Dr T. R. Wasule, professor of pathology, was delivering a series of lectures on brain tumours. His teaching style was such that a majority of the students developed headaches halfway through the lecture. In some, the intensity of the pain was so great that they suspected they had got brain tumours themselves. Junaid and Lazarus were in favour of bunking the class, but with JD and Mehul in the mood to attend and Manish throwing in the towel, they trudged back to the college building to attend Dr Wasule's lecture.

Junaid, Lazarus and Manish always sat as far back as they could, because some teachers had the unpleasant habit of demanding answers to their questions from students who were concentrating on the slender necks and silky hair of girls rather than the blackboard. By sitting at the back, it was possible to give the impression of overpowering concentration even if asleep. It was also convenient for making an exit unobtrusively when the lecture became insufferably boring.

JD's face lit up on seeing Mansi sitting alone in the front row. 'Have you come here straight from the obstetrics ward?' he asked, sitting down beside her.

'Yes, I was busy taking the history of a patient. By the way, Dr Veena Rao has informed us that we should go for the evening clinics regularly and try to attend as many deliveries as we can during our posting.'

'Don't tell me! Attending morning clinics is in itself a tough proposition. Spending the evenings inside that fish market is not my cup of tea,' JD was aghast.

'It's up to you, but I plan to attend the evening clinics.'

'In that case, I can reconsider my decision,' JD smiled sheepishly.

'Good for you,' Mansi smiled back.

At that point, Dr T. R. Wasule entered the classroom carrying a set of transparencies he wanted to teach by using the OHP (overhead projector). The students in the front rows stood up, while students behind them half-stood and the last few rows didn't bother to strain their muscles at all. Thirty minutes into the lecture, half the students were holding their heads as if they had brain tumors, the rest were blissfully asleep. But Dr Wasule went on and on...*wasuling* (extracting) his guru dakshina.

⊕

JD reached the obstetrics ward at 5.30 p.m., thirty minutes before the evening clinic was due to begin. He had put on his apron and his stetho hung prominently from his neck. These were important safeguards against denial of entry into the ward or eviction from the ward by a whimsical staff nurse or junior lady doctor. He had also applied a killer dose of Jōvan Musk for Men. The purpose was two-fold, to suppress the hospital smell and impress the girl he was smitten with.

JD peeped inside the labour room, hoping that Mansi might have arrived to observe the deliveries conducted by the residents. The overpowering stench of sweat, blood and urine laced with antiseptics and disinfectants made him feel like puking. The insides of the labour room were typical—dark, wet and rotting. A black cat sitting atop a steel almirah keenly eyed two fat rats scurrying around the sticky floor.

The labour room was practically empty except for a thin, pale, fragile woman lying on the labour table wearing a loose hospital gown. Her eyes tightly shut, teeth clenched, she was sweating profusely. It was obvious even to an untrained person like JD that she was in an advanced state of labour. This was thanks mainly to Bollywood movies in which the directors are so hung up on showing gory, protracted labour scenes in minute detail with the woman trying her best to blow away the roof of the cinema hall with her incessant shouting.

'Where the fuck is everyone?' JD spoke in a trembling, frightened voice.

'Oh, you have come, doctor,' the woman opened her eyes.

'Where the... Where is everyone?' JD repeated the question dropping the F-word. His lips quivered, fingers trembled, hands shook, legs shuddered, spine shivered, in fact his entire body shook like a lone coconut tree swaying in a thunderstorm ready to drop all its coconuts.

'I don't know, the young nurse rushed off to fetch a doctor when my labour pains started unexpectedly.'

'What do you mean by "unexpectedly"? Aren't you expected to get pains before you deliver?'

'My delivery was not expected for another six to eight hours, so everyone had gone out for a cup of tea, leaving me with that young, trainee nurse.'

'Now, what?' JD was like an actor who had forgotten his lines. 'Now...tell me, how many children do you have?'

'Three, doctor,' the woman groaned.

JD heaved a sigh of relief. At least one of them knew a bit about delivering babies.

The woman began to twist and turn frighteningly. 'I think it's coming, doctor!' she gasped, between her contractions.

JD grasped her hand tightly. 'You'll be all right in a minute,' he said, as confidently as possible. 'Leave it to...leave it to...' He couldn't bring himself to say 'leave it to me' so he finally said, 'Leave it to God!'

'I feel so sick!' the woman cried out in pain.

'So do I,' blurted JD.

There was, however, one standby that JD had thoughtfully taken the trouble to carry in his apron pocket. He turned his back towards the woman and slyly drew out a small but valuable book in a limp, black cover—*The Beginner's Obstetric Guide*. It was written by an Indian author who was under no illusion about the competence of medical students. It started off with 'The Normal Delivery'. The text was written in short, numbered paragraphs, keeping in mind the short attention span of present-day students.

JD glanced at the first page. 'ASEPSIS', it said. 'The person conducting the delivery must remember the five cleans—clean hands, clean cord, clean blade, clean thread and clean surroundings.' It went on to describe the importance of clean hands and how the person about to carry out a delivery should scrub up as thoroughly as for a surgical operation. At the bottom of the page there were diagrams showing the six steps of scrubbing.

'Scrubbing, that's it!' JD slipped the guide back into his apron pocket and went towards the washbasin. He picked up the gooey, half-melted soap from the rusted soap dish and started scrubbing.

'Oh, doctor, doctor…!' cried the woman.

'Don't get alarmed,' said JD tremulously.

'It's coming, doctor!'

JD scrubbed furiously.

The woman groaned loudly.

JD scrubbed even more vigorously.

The cat lost patience finally. It jumped down from its perch atop the almirah and the rats ran off.

Suddenly, JD became aware of a new note in the woman's cries—a louder, shriller continuous wailing followed by a muffled squeal and then, silence. He dropped the soap and looked back. The baby was coming out and there was no one to receive it! JD dived forwards and plucked the baby inches from the ground as it dangled precariously by its umbilical cord. The slimy thing almost slipped out of his hands but he held on to it for dear life. It was by far the best and the most important catch he had ever taken (and JD had taken quite a few in the slips).

JD stood up with the baby secure in his arms and showed it to the mother. 'It's a baby boy,' he declared after carefully checking the baby's genitals.

She looked at it lovingly. 'Do you deliver a lot of babies, doctor?'

'Hundreds,' JD said confidently. 'Every day.'

'What's your name, doctor, if you don't mind?'

'Jai.'

'I'll name him after you,' the woman said with sincerity.

Precisely at that moment, Dr Veena Rao and two senior

nurses entered the labour room with the young trainee nurse in tow. They saw JD and the woman talking comfortably to each other, with the newborn crying lustily in JD's arms.

'Good work, Mr...?' Dr Rao hesitated.

'Jai Dhawan,' supplied JD.

'Oh, I am very happy that you are so interested in learning obstetrics,' said Dr Rao taking the baby from JD.

JD beamed and bowed graciously. He was genuinely proud of the child born through his own efforts. In the flattering atmosphere, he had already forgotten that his single manoeuvre in effecting the delivery was successfully catching the baby before it hit the ground. It had more to do with his good cricketing skills than his excellent knowledge of obstetrics.

One of the nurses cut and clamped the baby's cord. She wiped the baby gently with cotton gauge and wrapped him in a clean white sheet and placed him beside the mother. Before leaving, JD looked back one final time and felt a sense of peace when he saw the woman with her little baby sleeping contentedly in the crook of her arm. JD felt the name of the medical profession had never stood higher.

13
Can I Hold Your Hand?

JD was now well recognized in the ObG department. After all, it isn't every day that a mere medical student, on the very first day, in his maiden posting, successfully conducts a delivery, entirely by his own efforts! No one asked and JD told nobody what exactly happened.

During one evening clinic, after showing the students a complicated breech delivery, Dr Veena Rao announced that she was going on leave for three days. 'I'll try to see that somebody takes your clinics but I'm not sure... The workload is heavy and some other residents are also on leave.'

Fortunately, for so many overworked postgraduate students, three holidays had fallen on consecutive dates. Saturday, 13 August, was Raksha Bandhan; the fourteenth a Sunday; and Monday, 15 August, was a national holiday. It was a rare combination and one where even the most khadoos HOD would have found it extremely difficult to deny leave to some of the PG students.

Twenty-eight-year-old Dr Veena Rao had been married for more than two years. Her husband, Rajshekhar Rao, was doing his MD in medicine from the Government Medical College, Nagrajpur. Shuttling between Bhopla and Nagrajpur was how the two young doctors spent their holidays—their marriage consisting of brief, stolen moments of bliss followed by endless, tiring hours of hospital work. What an absolutely fabulous way to build the foundation of your future married life! If a movie on relationships was made in today's time, it would be titled *Love in Transit* or maybe *Love by Satellite*.

But that is what a doctor's life is, marked by—compromises, sacrifices and hardships. Forget about courtship and try not to land in front of your lordship in a consumer court. Someone had rightly put up a poster in the common room of the PG hostel:

R U—

- Psychologically numbed?
- Mentally starved?
- Creatively challenged?
- Artistically void?
- Socially outcast?
- Emotionally blackmailed?

Congratulations!

U R—

A DOCTOR

In the mornings, the students were asked to tag along during the consultant's round, but as expected, no one was available to take the evening clinics. The students heaved a sigh of relief—an escape from studies is always welcome during the phase when your only job is to study. The students were left to their own devices but were basically supposed to write down the case histories of the patients allotted to them. Boys never really bothered to take down any case histories while many girls also avoided it. It was a well-known fact that for the past thirty years of its existence, only the first batch of the Nehru Medical College had noted down the medical histories of the ObG patients. Year after year the same Ramwatis, Rampyaris and Ramdularis kept appearing on the pages of the patient-history notebooks with the same complaints, same treatments and same results.

Mansi and one or two other girls still came to the wards regularly but others, especially the boys, were having a great time malling, cineplexing and birdwatching—though not necessarily in that order. One evening JD ditched the gang and came to the ObG wards to check out on Mansi. He found her in the postnatal ward talking to the matron in charge of the ward. The matron stared at him with unbridled hostility, but as he came closer she recognized him.

'Oh, it's the laiding aabstrician of the batch, Mr Yedi,' the matron announced in her heavy South Indian accent. Even after spending forty years in Central India, it was as if she had never left the backwaters of Kerala.

'Good evening, matron. Hi, Mansi!' JD smiled disarmingly.

'So you are heaaar to learn about the post-parrrtum cazes,' the matron looked from JD to Mansi and back with a thick-lipped smile. It was plainly obvious why JD was there, with no apron, no stetho and no notebook or pen on his person.

JD and Mansi's obvious discomfiture was relieved by the arrival of a young couple at the ward entrance.

'Aaammmaaa,' the dark, fat belle with long hair, well oiled and neatly braided, called out to the matron. One look at the young woman's hair, and the Indian Oil Corporation would have agreed on a twenty-five-year lease to extract oil from her hair. She had a mini jasmine garden on top of her head. The short, wiry guy beside her looked as if he hadn't had a decent meal in his entire life.

'Aiaeeyo Ponamma…you wait right there, I am coming.' The matron's face lit up on seeing the duo. 'My daater and son-in-law…' she said, as she turned with surprising speed for her bulk, and rushed off in their direction.

'What were you discussing with the matron?' JD asked Mansi, relieved to get some privacy.

'Oh, nothing much. She was complaining about her workload, her arthritis, her gallstones and the wayward ways of the younger lot of nurses.'

'The usual cribbing a person does at that age,' observed JD.

'Not exactly, she made a very pertinent point. She seemed to be really annoyed with the government's decision to raise the retirement age for the nursing staff to sixty-five.'

'Why? I suppose most people would be happy that they can work for a few more years.' JD showed his surprise.

Mansi shook her head. 'She said that the government has not taken the decision to benefit the medical staff. There is an acute shortage of trained nurses, paramedical staff and doctors in the government-run institutions. The government just keeps raising the retirement age to overcome the shortfall without realizing the consequences. Working in a hospital is not like working in the secretariat where bada babus and chhota babus, the bureaucrats, just keep sitting on the files, delaying decisions and taking bribes. Whenever one goes there to meet somebody the fellow is invariably in a meeting and still nothing ever gets done.'

'It's true that hospital work is quite taxing, you have to be on your toes always,' JD remarked caustically. 'You can't sit back in air-conditioned comfort over a cup of coffee and work for the larger benefit of a larger number of people as our bureaucrats do.' He looked at his wristwatch. 'Are you done with your ward work or do you want to stay a bit longer?'

'No, I was on my way when the matron caught hold of me.'

'Good! If you don't have any specific plans, can we go out for dinner?'

'Dinner? But…won't we get late?'

'Not at all. There is a nice little place nearby called Panjabiyat where the food is really good and the service fast. You will be back in the hostel within an hour.'

'I don't know...' Mansi sounded hesitant.

'Oh come on, I am sure you too are fed up with the insipid hostel food, or do they serve gourmet delights in your mess?'

Mansi made a face. 'The food in the girls' hostel mess is terrible. It's much worse than what it is in the boys' mess. There they don't give a damn whereas in the boys' hostel they always have the fear of getting bashed up if they serve shitty food.'

'So it's decided then, let's go to Panjabiyat,' JD grinned.

'Okay, Panjabiyat it is,' said Mansi.

They came out of the ward and rode off on JD's Hero Honda Splendor NXG.

Patrons of Panjabiyat, a thriving little restaurant in the busy Indira Market area, were mostly people interested in Indian vegetarian delicacies. JD selected a table in the far corner of the hall partially hidden behind a pillar. Behaving like a true gentleman, he pulled back the chair for Mansi and helped her sit comfortably. He hesitated for a moment, debating whether to sit beside her or on the opposite side. Then planning his innings for a Test match, he sat down opposite her. He was sure there would be many occasions in the near future when he would be able to sit next to her.

'What should we order?' JD asked, picking up the menu placed in front of him by the waiter.

'It's your call, you seem to know the place well.'

'Okay,' agreed JD. 'Whenever our family goes out for dinner, my mom does the ordering. You know why?'

'Tell me.'

'Because if my father places the order, we end up with enough food on our table to last us a whole week.'

Mansi laughed her tinkling laugh. JD felt as if a guitar has been plucked deep inside his heart. It almost killed him.

JD kept looking at Mansi, unable to take his eyes off her beautiful face. Black suited her. She was wearing an embroidered black top with black jeans and it complemented her extremely fair complexion tremendously. The waiter coughed discreetly, quite enjoying the scene. JD came out of his trance and focused on the menu.

'Which soup would you prefer, hot and sour or cream of tomato?' he asked Mansi.

'Hot and sour.'

'Two hot and sour soups,' JD told the waiter.

'No, make it one-by-two,' Mansi intervened.

'Okay, also one Potato 65, one Paneer Pasanda and three butter naans,' JD completed the order.

'Green salad, raita, papad?' asked the waiter, aiming to inflate the bill.

'No!' JD said firmly. He wasn't that blind to fall in the trap, even with a blindingly beautiful girl with him. Moreover, he knew the hotel served free onions and pickle, so where was the need to dole out an extra fifty-sixty bucks?

'Do you want anything to drink while you wait for your order?' the waiter made a last-ditch effort.

'Yes, two chilled Pepsis!' JD relented.

'Make it one, we will share it. I want to enjoy the food,' remarked Mansi.

With the ordering done and over with, they leaned back in their seats and tried to soak in the atmosphere. It was apparent the restaurant was doing quite well as most of tables were occupied. There was cheerful banter all around, proving that the food was wholesome and tasted good.

'You were telling me about your family, so tell me some more,' Mansi prodded JD.

'Oh, I've a younger brother who is in the third semester at DCE, that's the Delhi College of Engineering. My father works for Ogilvy and Mather, the multinational advertising agency. My mother is a housewife.'

'So your father must be travelling abroad quite frequently.'

'No, hardly. He is in the finance department.' JD poured half the Pepsi in a glass for Mansi and took a large swig from the bottle. 'What about your family?'

'I, too, have one brother who is five years older than me. He has BTech and MBA degrees and is employed with Accenture. My father is a banker and my mother is a university teacher.'

The waiter placed the soup bowls in front of Mansi and JD along with a basket of buns and soup-sticks.

'I love soup-sticks,' said Mansi, warming up to the appetizing smell of warm soup.

'I prefer buns,' said JD, dipping one into his soup bowl.

'Gosh! Their hot and sour soup is really hot and I don't mean its temperature,' Mansi dropped the spoon back into the bowl.

'Bite on your soup-stick and give it a second try. I think you will like it.'

'I want to, it's very tasty, but I am not used to so much mirchi.'

After an attempt or two, Mansi gave up on her soup, but JD polished it off with great relish.

'You really have a great liking for hot stuff,' Mansi remarked innocently.

'That I do,' JD looked at Mansi mischievously.

Mansi picked up her spoon threateningly. 'Why do you boys always have to give everything a double meaning? Why do you guys specialize in thinking dirty?'

'Aren't girls responsible for keeping our dirty minds ticking?

Why do they pluck their eyebrows, paint their lips, apply mascara, use eye shadow. What are tight tops and low-waisted jeans for? To look like Mother Teresa?'

'I must congratulate you for your exhaustive knowledge of cosmetics. How many girlfriends did it take to learn all this?'

Before the argument could proceed any further, the waiter arrived with the rest of their order. The food was extremely tasty and both of them tore into it with gusto.

'This dish, Potato 69 or whatever, is out of this world,' said Mansi, gulping down a deep-red chunky piece.

'It's Potato 65, and yes, it would be equally fantastic even if it was named Potato 165 or 185,' said JD, shovelling in some more.

The waiter came up again and removed the empty dishes. 'Any sweets, some ice cream?'

JD pushed the menu towards Mansi. 'Do you want some ice cream?'

Mansi looked at the desserts section of the menu briefly. 'What they are charging for a measly slice of stale ice cream can buy us a whole brick. Forget about it,' she said with finality.

'Maybe on our way back we can stop at the Neel Sagar Lake for ice cream. We only have to make a small detour for it.' JD saw and grabbed his opportunity. He wanted to be with Mansi for as long as possible.

'Okay. I think we can do that,' said Mansi, looking at her wristwatch.

'Just get us the bill,' JD told the waiter.

The waiter ambled off, not looking awfully impressed by the miserly manner in which the two had ordered. He had an uncomfortable feeling that his tip was going to be severely compromised.

'Can I have your cell number?' JD asked with some trepidation.

'Wait,' said Mansi, picking up her cell phone. 'Tell me your number and I'll give you a missed call.'

The tune of *'Tere mast mast do nain...'* rang out from JD's phone. He pressed the call reject key and saved the number. But instead of Mansi's name, he entered the word 'Dil', heart. Then on the spur of moment he switched off his phone so no calls could disturb them.

The waiter returned in a few minutes with the bill enclosed in a leather folder with frayed edges and placed it before JD.

'We will share the cost of the meal,' said Mansi firmly.

'No, let this remain my treat. You can pay next time.'

'Very smart! By not letting me share the bill you have already ensured another dinner date with me.' Mansi started to laugh and JD joined in. This time his heart didn't play any tricks, it just kept beating lubb-dup, lubb-dup...

They reached the Neel Sagar Lake and purchased Chocobars from a Vadilal kiosk. Before JD could pull out his wallet from his hip pocket, Mansi had already paid the exact amount at the counter.

JD and Mansi started to walk on the paved pathway along the waterfront. There were not many people around, it being a weekday. They sat down on a bench looking at the lake water shimmering in the moonlight. The cool breeze, the gentle lapping of waves and the radiant full moon suspended in a cloudless sky is the stuff that inspires romance, poetry, longing and belonging. Mansi and JD kept sitting on the bench as if in a trance.

JD looked up at the moon and sighed. It was equally difficult to touch both the one in the sky and that on the earth sitting beside him. Now his heart started to play tricks again, accelerating, going faster and faster, totally out of his control. He turned and looked at Mansi. His heart did a somersault, threatening to come all the way out of his mouth.

'God she is beautiful!' he thought for the nth time.

Mansi became conscious of JD's gaze. 'What are you are looking at with that bemused look in your face?' she asked, fully aware of where he was looking.

JD couldn't reply, the words got lost, his breath got stuck and his heart went berserk.

After a few moments, JD steeled himself and asked softly, 'Mansi, can I hold your hand?'

Now it was Mansi who couldn't reply—the words got lost, her breath got stuck and her heart went berserk.

JD waited for what appeared an eternity but actually was only a few moments, then he took Mansi's hand in his and held it ever so gently. Mansi didn't resist, she didn't pull it back, she did nothing. Then suddenly she tightened her fingers and grasped JD's hand firmly. They kept sitting on the bench, holding hands, talking with their fingers, conversing with their nails, loving with the moistness of their palms and bonding with the firmness of their grasp.

Who said you needed to talk? Your touch can speak too, even more eloquently; you just need to fall in love.

JD leaned towards Mansi and gently put his lips on hers. Mansi let them linger there for a moment and then turned her face to the other side.

'I don't want to start something I can't stop,' she said, unsure of her feelings for JD.

14

FOSLA King

When JD returned after dropping Mansi, a party was going on in his room. Junaid, Lazarus, Mehul and Manish were eating biryani brought by Junaid from his home. A half-empty two-litre 7UP bottle stood on the table.

'Where the hell were you? I have been trying to call you the entire evening, but your mobile was switched off,' complained Junaid.

JD took out his mobile from his jeans pocket and switched it on. 'The bloody thing is giving trouble. It sometimes switches off automatically.'

The truth was that JD had switched off his mobile in the restaurant. He didn't want to be disturbed when he was with Mansi. Yes, girls can make you lie to your best friends, but who cares? Surely not JD—he found Mansi irresistible, so friends and friendships could wait.

'Ammi had prepared mutton biryani and asked me to call you guys over. When I couldn't contact you, I packed it and brought it to your room,' Junaid was still a bit uptight.

'You could have waited for me,' JD protested.

'We waited for close to two hours, but you were untraceable,' Lazarus tried to suck out the marrow from a hollow bone.

'Have some, there is plenty more,' Junaid pushed a bowl in front of JD.

JD couldn't resist the intoxicating aroma of biryani and in spite of already having had dinner, polished off all the contents of the bowl.

'Oh, a private party is going on without informing friends right next door,' Bhavesh Mehta barged in, grinning ear-to-ear.

'If you want to eat, there is still plenty left, Bhavesh Bhai,' Lazarus thrust the bone he was holding in Bhavesh's face.

Bhavesh jumped back, almost falling in JD's lap. 'Don't try to act over smart. You know I am pure veg,' he said, still smiling.

'What's the matter, man, you look like a dog with a bone,' Manish pulled Bhavesh's leg.

'A juicy bone would have been more appropriate,' Bhavesh smacked his lips. 'I met Minal in the market this evening and we had ice cream together,' his voice acquired a conspiratorial tone.

'*Saale chhupe rustam*, you dark horse! That calls for a treat,' Manish backslapped Bhavesh.

'All in good time, all in good time, let me first find out her true feelings for me.' The businessman in Bhavesh Bhai was unwilling to dole out a dime before making sure of the profits.

And that is how a new recruit joined the FOSLA! He had the attributes—he was gullible, he was stupid, he was tenacious, and he was crazy about Minal.

He had just shared an ice cream with Minal and he was already making plans to hook her. He had one-sidedly acquired a 50 per cent stake in the relationship without the other party even knowing it.

'I hope you didn't let her pay for the ice cream,' commented Mehul sarcastically. He was looking a bit upset, but he didn't know exactly why. He liked Minal but was not sure of his feelings for her. Probably he didn't like the way these guys were talking about Minal.

'How could I let that happen!' said Bhavesh vainly. 'Two orange bars cost just ten bucks.'

'Bhencho, you fed her an orange bar and are now waiting to find out her true feelings,' Junaid was appalled. 'If I were Minal I would have thrown a five-rupee coin in your face and walked off.'

'She insisted upon having an orange bar, so what could have I done?' Bhavesh was close to tears.

'You fool, next time a girl like Minal lets you buy an ice cream, rush to Pundhra, Gujarat, and buy her the Vadilal factory. I know your diamond merchant baap is quite capable of doing that,' Lazarus came up with some serious advice.

Bhavesh appeared devastated. He looked appealingly from JD to Manish to Junaid to Lazarus searching for some gyan. He firmly believed that you didn't need a Bodh Vriksh to get enlightenment. Your buddies and not Buddha will prove to be your saviour.

'How did she look at you when you two were sucking on your orange bars?' Junaid asked.

'*Uski palkein jhuki-jhuki theen,*' replied Bhavesh poetically, perhaps wishfully thinking that Minal had lowered her eyelids coyly.

'She definitely doesn't suffer from ptosis (drooping of the upper eyelid), so the downcast eyes mean she was acutely aware of you,' concluded Lazarus.

'What was the colour of her eyes?' Junaid enquired.

'Somewhat red.'

'As she is not suffering from conjunctivitis, her eyes must have become red because she was feeling shy. Another positive for you, man!' Lazarus grinned roguishly.

'Now tell me, in between sucking on her orange bar, did she look at you with tirchi nazar?' Junaid questioned in all seriousness.

'I think, yes. She did squint a little at me once or twice.'

'Minal doesn't have a squint. So she was stealing quick glances at you. Positive again,' observed Lazarus.

'Did you look at her hand, the one she was holding the orange bar with? Was it shaking? Were there any tremors?' Junaid inquired like a real doctor.

'Yes. Her hand did shake a bit.'

'Minal is young, so Parkinson's disease is ruled out. Dude, you were causing her hand to shake. A big positive.' Lazarus patted Bhavesh encouragingly.

'Now one last question, Bhavesh. Do you see her face all around you? I mean like in that song *"Har taraf tera chehra..."* Junaid tried to look very concerned.

'I don't know, maybe yes.'

'You are not suffering from hallucinations, so it is a sure sign of love.' Lazarus came to a final diagnosis.

Bhavesh was reasonably impressed with the systematic approach adopted by Junaid and Lazarus. The medical terms like ptosis, conjunctivitis, squint, hallucinations and Parkinson's disease overwhelmed him. The duo succeeded in convincing him that he was in love although he himself had no such thought before coming to JD's room.

Mehul didn't like the whole conversation and remained largely quiet during the entire drama. He was confused about whether he liked Minal or disliked Bhavesh liking her.

'JD Bhai, please tell me what to do,' Bhavesh became senti.

JD remained quiet. He didn't much believe in setting up people and although Bhavesh wasn't a close friend, he wasn't an enemy either.

Bhavesh came near JD and held his hands. 'Please tell me how to impress Minal,' he pleaded.

Trapped into emotional blackmail, JD didn't have much choice. 'Girls like dashing boys riding jazzy bikes. I think you should abandon your Scooty and get an Avenger.'

Bhavesh didn't understand what Avenger meant. 'You know

a lot about bikes, JD, please tell me which one should I buy?'

'Avenger 220 DTS-i is the name of a stylish bike manufactured by Bajaj Auto,' Junaid laughed.

'This fool will never be able to hook a girl,' butted in Lazarus.

'Don't be so mean,' JD rebuked Junaid and Lazarus, trying very hard to suppress a smile.

'I will show you what I am capable of, you jokers.' Bhavesh was beside himself with rage.

'Bhavesh, cool down, they didn't mean any harm. It's in their nature—they can't remain serious for more than five minutes.'

'I am warning you, you two…' Bhavesh pointed at Junaid and Lazarus ominously.

'Chill, Bhavesh, you have already called them jokers and that's what they are,' intervened JD.

'I'll see their faces when Minal takes a lift on my Revenger. Bloody monkeys.' Bhavesh stomped out of the room, his face contorted with rage.

'It's Avenger, Bhavesh Bhai, not Revenger,' Junaid and Lazarus shouted in tandem.

'There was no need to provoke him, yaar,' said JD, draining the last drop from the 7UP bottle.

'Who asked him to barge in and brag about treating Minal to an orange bar? I certainly didn't,' smirked Junaid, still quite pleased with the job well done.

'How foolish can you all get? Fighting over what? Fighting for what? On one side you have Bhavesh deciding unilaterally on acquiring a 50 per cent stake in a relationship with Minal. On the other side, Minal, who holds the remaining 50 per cent is not even aware of the whole bloody thing. And these two Narad Munis are doing their best to add fuel to the fire,' Mehul finally decided to speak up.

'I think Mehul is right. Now you two, just keep away from

Bhavesh. Try not to complicate things any further; JD tried to drill some sense into Junaid and Lazarus.

A quick recap about FOSLA:

- ⇢ The male partner exercises a firm control over his 50 per cent of shares (not allowing others to even talk to the girl)
- ⇢ The female partner has a 50 per cent stake but is totally unaware of it and
- ⇢ The share-brokers (that is the minimally involved guys, because no guy is uninvolved where girls are concerned) laugh away to glory

⊕

After a week, Bhavesh Bhai's gleaming black and chrome Avenger 220 DTS-i was parked provocatively right at the entrance of the UG hostel. Impressed onlookers surrounding the bike were being treated to khamand and dhokla especially ordered from Narmada Sweets. The Avenger had a marigold garland around its headlight and a red satiya marked on its petrol tank. A big teeka adorned the forehead of Bhavesh Bhai. He was beaming with pride as if the garland was not around the Avenger's headlight but encircling Minal's delicate neck.

Bhavesh invited JD to take a trial ride as a token of appreciation for suggesting a bike supremely worthy of riding around with Minal. The fellow had not given even a second's thought to the possibility of Minal's refusal. He surely had an F chromosome, absolutely necessary to be a FOSLA member, in his genetic make-up. Later, several seniors and some opportunistic juniors also took joyrides sitting behind Bhavesh Bhai. It irritated him greatly as in his mind the seat had already been reserved for Minal. Permanently!

Every evening, Bhavesh would get into his Levis (which he

pronounced Lay-vis), black T-shirt and white Reeboks. God only knows how old his deo was because it smelled worse than the fumes coming out of the Avenger's exhaust. Then he would self-start his bike and pass in front of the girls' hostel every thirty minutes until it was dark. His routine was so predictable that the day-shift watchman standing guard at the hostel gate started to prepare to go home when Bhavesh arrived on the third round.

Finally, Lady Luck smiled on Bhavesh Bhai and his dream-girl came to stand on the balcony. While passing in front of the hostel, Bhavesh saw Minal leaning from the balcony of her second-floor room, talking to some girls standing on the ground below. He slowed the bike and, using the clutch and accelerator combo, revved up the engine. Minal looked in his direction. Bhavesh waved and Minal waved back, smiling radiantly. Bhavesh kept waving, and waving, and...

While waving, Bhavesh had lifted his hand from the clutch, but had forgotten to release the accelerator from his grip. The powerful Avenger bike literally took off. Bhavesh was still looking at Minal, his neck rotated to its maximum. The road curved sharply to right. A nullah flowed along the left side of the road. The Avenger left the tarmac and dived into the nullah, disturbing a peace-loving family of pigs eating a leisurely dinner. Bhavesh sank into the deep muck with his bike on top of him and two piglets under him.

The crash was so loud that half the girls' hostel was out on the balconies in a flash. The watchman came running and saw Bhavesh lying in the nullah. While he was trying to escape from below the bike, the two piglets were attempting to wriggle out from underneath him. In spite of the gravity of the situation, the watchman couldn't stop himself from laughing out aloud.

'*Arre, daksaab, kya hua?*'

'*Saale gadhe, dikh...nahi...raha! Aaahh!*' Bhavesh winced in pain. '*Katrina aur Kareena ke saath bathtub mein naha raha hoon.*' But even in this state he looked in the direction of the balcony. He momentarily wondered if Minal would come rushing down to help him before he passed out in a daze.

It would have warmed his heart to know that it was Minal who called up the hospital emergency line. An ambulance arrived in a few minutes and Bhavesh was taken out of the nullah. He was admitted to the orthopaedic ward with fourteen fractures. The tibia, fibula, radius, ulna, four ribs on the left side along with humerus, and two ribs on the right were broken. Three small bones of the left wrist joint—the scaphoid, lunate and triquetral—were also fractured, making a grand total of fourteen. These three small bones were the ones he had so painstakingly memorized during the first professional exam with the help of the mnemonic, *Suman Lata Tinde Paka, Tinde Tere Kachche Hain*. Alas, Suman Lata's tindas remained uncooked!

What an irony it was that now, with fourteen broken bones, there was absolutely no possibility of his taking Minal out on 14 February, Valentine's Day, which was just round the corner.

⊕

A week later, when Bhavesh had recovered sufficiently to be able to sit propped up in bed, a delegation comprising Prem Arora (undeclared president of FOSLA), Mannu Sharma (Gestapo representative), some prominent seniors (including Danav Sisodia) and a few of his batchmates (Junaid, Lazarus, Mehul and others) visited the orthopaedic ward late in the evening. Jignesh, Bhavesh's younger brother who had arrived from Kutch in Gujarat, sat on a wooden stool beside the bed. He and Bhavesh looked warily at the group approaching them.

Junaid moved up ahead of the group and waved cheerily. On reaching the bed, he leaned forwards and delicately hugged

Bhavesh, giving full respect to his fourteen broken bones.

'How are you doing, man?' he asked, tapping the plaster on Bhavesh's left leg.

'I am all right, except for the pain and the intense itching.'

Junaid wanted to say this intense itching was the result of another kind of intense itching, the one which caused Bhavesh to dream of giving Minal a lift on his bike, but he kept quiet—no point in hurting an already injured guy.

'I am also sick of piddling in the urine-pot and shitting in the bedpan,' Bhavesh continued further.

'Don't worry, in a few days' time, you will be able to sit on a chair with a hole in the centre and then you can piss and shit in peace.' Junaid tried to console Bhavesh in his own funny style.

Lazarus came up and whispered something in Jignesh's ear, making him disappear immediately. 'Bhavesh Bhai, all these seniors have especially come to meet you,' he said, inviting the group to come near the bed.

Prem Arora, the undeclared president of FOSLA, shuffled forward and looked admiringly at the innumerable signatures adorning the plaster on Bhavesh's body. He was so overcome with emotion that he had to clear his choked throat repeatedly. 'We are here to show solidarity with you and your cause. You have gained a whole lot of admirers in the college by this one brave act of yours. It takes a lot of courage and conviction to ride the Avenger 200 DTS-i at close to 80 kilometres per hour while simultaneously waving at a girl standing on the second-floor balcony of the girls' hostel.'

'Yes, you have risen greatly in our collective esteem. You have our full sympathies and wholehearted support,' said Mannu Sharma, ruffling Bhavesh's hair lovingly.

Bhavesh smiled uncertainly not knowing what to say. What these buggers were calling bravery, JD had termed as committing suicide. But how could all these fellows be wrong? Agreed. they were jilted lovers, losers where girls were concerned, but that was not the only dimension to their life. Some of them were brilliant sportsmen, others were good in studies and certainly, all of them were going to become doctors and cure patients. Slowly, Bhavesh's smile widened till most of his thirty-two teeth were fully exposed. Yes indeed, it was an act of daredevilry and he was a hero who deserved the admiration of his peers.

'Thank you, thanks a lot,' said Bhavesh shyly. 'It means a lot to me. But I am really worried about my studies, especially my attendance, as I am bound to miss a lot of classes in the next two to three months.'

'Don't worry. *Arre tu bhaai hai re hamara*. You're our brother. We will see to it that demonstrators and young assistant professors, most of whom are also like brothers to us (thereby meaning present or past frustoos = FOSLA members), will help you during the practicals as well as the theory papers. As far as attendance is concerned, a concerted effort will be launched to get you proxy attendance,' assured Prem Arora, still very animated. He was passing out of NMC in a few months. Now he could leave his alma mater secure in the knowledge that a worthy successor for the title of the FOSLA King had arrived on the horizon, although 'crash-landed in the nullah' would have been more appropriate.

The Avenger 200 DTS-i was fished out of the nullah and dumped near the boys' hostel gate. It went to rust gradually, its paint fading slowly and the chrome losing its shine. Grass and weeds started to cover it, turning it into a forgotten war memorial of an unknown soldier. Some crafty hosteller wrote an epitaph on the Avenger's petrol tank:

Here lies the bike of Bhavesh Bhai
Undisputed FOSLA KING

15

FOSLA Celebrates Valentine's Day

For our frustoos, Valentine's Day is the most important day and St Valentine the most revered and sacred saint. The day does have some magical, some ethereal quality to it because over the years a few frustoos did finally manage to get hitched on 14 February. Is it magic? Is it love? No one knows for sure, but there is some lust-chemical in the air on this day.

Prem Arora, the undeclared president of FOSLA, was highly active on this day. If Newton had seen his energy levels, he would surely have propounded the fourth law of energy: the magnetic energy produced by a girl is directly proportional to the number of boys circulating in her orbit. Since the arrival of Prem Arora, FOSLA had flourished in NMC. Prem had given his blood, sweat (and more) to the organization and it had grown from strength to strength.

The boys' hostel was abuzz a day prior to Valentine's Day. Understandably, there was visible excitement all around. Many boys had broken their sacred oath of not bathing from December to March. Soap, shampoo and perfume were being used liberally. The atmosphere in the girls' hostel was relatively sombre. Most of the girls were either indifferent or feigned indifference to St Valentine's memory. Girls with boyfriends (a very small group) were expectedly busy. They had been discussing what dress to wear on the 'V' day. Once that was decided, matching accessories were collected from different rooms.

JD tried calling Mansi several times on the thirteenth evening but couldn't get through to her. Each time, the recorded message he received was either 'the phone is switched off' or 'moved out of coverage area'. JD knew it wasn't the case. Actually there was a signal problem in and around the girls' hostel, which had put paid to the aspirations of several prospective FOSLA members. Finally, around 9 p.m., JD got Mansi on the line.

'Hi!' Mansi's voice rang out from the phone and JD forgot all the accumulated frustration of the evening.

'What's up?' asked JD, trying to control his excitement.

'Nothing much, just had dinner and came out to the front courtyard for a stroll with Minal.' There was a slight husky undertone in Mansi's voice which JD found irresistible.

'I've been trying to call you all evening without luck,' complained JD.

'Well, you've turned lucky just now, to be precise, at 9.15 p.m.,' said Mansi teasingly.

'Agreed, I am lucky and blessed to have you...'

There was absolute silence on Mansi's side.

'...to have you on the other side of the phone line,' completed JD slowly.

'Tell me, why did you want to talk to me so desperately?' Mansi's silken voice floated out of JD's phone.

'Try to make an intelligent guess!' JD smiled into the phone. Now that he was talking to Mansi, his desperation was gone. Except for the fluttering of his heart, he was in sound health.

'I am not good at guessing games. Tell me what's on your mind.'

'What's the date tomorrow?'

'You have called me to find out the date?' Mansi knew the date and its importance but decided to act coy.

'Don't play that game with me. I know you are far too intelligent not to understand what I am talking about.'

'Someone is getting upset unnecessarily,' said Mansi mockingly.

'Don't get me wrong. The signal drops so frequently in your hostel that I fear I won't be able to complete what I want to say.'

'Okay, tell me what's on your mind.' Mansi knew why JD had called, but girls always want it spelled out. They want the boys to plead and grovel.

'Can we go out on a date tomorrow?' JD asked a bit awkwardly.

Mansi remained quiet for a while. She understood fully well the meaning of going out on a date on Valentine's Day. It was like confirming a relationship and Mansi was not ready for that. Although she liked JD and was attracted to him, getting into a serious commitment was not what she wanted.

'Hey, are you there?' JD asked in a concerned voice. He thought the connection had snapped.

'Yeah, I am listening.'

'Let's meet tomorrow. We can catch a movie or maybe go out for dinner again.'

'So you want to gain parity real quick. You're afraid that I will forget about my return treat,' Mansi laughed in her inimitable style, making JD's heart do a somersault.

'It's nothing of the sort. I just wanted to be with you. Alone!'

'JD, why don't you understand? If people see us together on a 'V' day date, they will put things in a wrong perspective. They will attach a label to our friendship. I don't want that to happen.'

'Listen, Mansi, I care about you a lot and I don't want any loose talk to affect you. We can just go for a ride on my bike together and grab a pizza at Domino's and be back before it's dark,' JD persisted.

Mansi dithered for a few seconds but finally consented to JD's proposal. 'Okay, I'll meet you near the college gate at 5 p.m.'

If JD hadn't been standing on the third floor of the boys' hostel, he would have surely jumped down on the ground with happiness. Instead he dashed into his room and did an impromptu jig standing on his bed. Getting down from the bed, he went straight towards the mirror fixed on the wall. He tilted his head to the right and gave a slight jerk backwards, flicking the tuft of hair on his forehead back—à la Shammi Kapoor. Then he gave half a smile and spent the next few minutes in front of the mirror appreciating his good looks.

He may be forgiven this display of vanity since the BLT (Beauty List Topper) of the batch had agreed to go on a date with him.

⊕

Like every year on the night of 13 February, around midnight a baraat of frustoos started from the boys' hostel towards the girls' hostel. Although several prominent FOSLA members were a part of the baraat, Prem Arora was the undisputed groom (with his rich experience of at least twelve rejections). A few days earlier, after the latest debacle when Mannu Sharma teased him, he boasted that he was a derby horse and would ultimately win the grand prize. To which Mannu had replied, 'Bhencho, forget about the prize, you will just keep running without ever being able to finish the race.'

The baraat started from the UG hostel and first went to the PG hostel to pick up its honourable members. Some of the baraatis were a little drunk but most were stoned. On reaching the gates of the girls' hostel the boys raised a huge war cry: *Bholay ke bhai bum, Bholay ke bhai bum, Bholay ke bhai bum, Bum Bholaay. Hari har, Hari har, Hari har.*

Prem Arora and Danav Sisodia broke into the song 'Character dheela hai...'

The organizers of the baraat had caught hold of a drummer for a princely sum of ₹50. The dark, skinny lad was beating the drum to the best of his limited capacity. The dancing began and some of the more daring frustoos climbed the roof of the pump-house located near the boundary wall of the girls' hostel. Their drunk, writhing motions were highlighted by the powerful halogen lamp atop the pump-house.

One by one, many more frustoos climbed up on the small roof of the pump-house pushing and elbowing each other, trying to remain in the light of the halogen lamp. The purpose was to be seen by the girls watching from the balconies and windows of the girls' hostel. Who knows, some of the more impressionable ones might fall for the bravehearts dancing on the rooftop! Such was the optimism of the boys.

Soon the malnourished drummer got tired and the dancing beat petered down to a slow drum roll for the martyrs. Prem Arora jumped forward and landed a resounding kick on his butt. He snatched the drum, hung it from his neck and started to hit it with a stick in a drunken stupor. Some senior girl on the balcony tittered, 'Hey, see now the groom is also the bandmaster of the baraat.'

Very few in the baraat had 'someone' special tucked away in the hostel, so they were naturally keeping a low profile. The majority didn't have 'anyone' in the hostel and they were shouting each other's name at the top of their voices. The strategy was simple—to let the girls know they were out there and available.

The two security guards deployed at the gate were glaring down at the boys with much malevolence, especially the one with a Veerappan-like moustache. From his grim expression, it was plainly obvious that he wouldn't even allow a dog to run away with a bitch, so a boy trying to elope with a girl stood no chance.

A unique aspect of the Valentine's Day celebrations was the burning of an effigy in front of the girls' hostel. This effigy was not of any particular person, but of the 'mindset' that girls have of not getting pataoed. It was a form of protest against the girls' tendency to give no lift to the boys even though the poor fellows had invested forty to fifty thousand of their fathers' hard-earned money in buying jazzy bikes with comfy pillion seats.

The effigy had been readied under the direct supervision of Riyaaz Mamu and at least ten to fifteen juniors had slogged the whole of the previous night making it. The final product would have made any modern sculptor proud. No one could really tell what it was and what it really depicted, if anything at all. The only smart thing about it was that it had three legs, which could be spread to form a tripod. This made the job of making the effigy stand on the ground absolutely hassle free. Among loud cheering, whistling and catcalls, the effigy was placed right in front of the girls' hostel gates by the baraatis and the groom was called to set it on fire.

'Fuck, man! I've forgotten to bring the matchbox.' Prem Arora looked disgustedly at Danav.

'Even I don't have one. Has anyone got a matchbox or a lighter?' hollered Danav.

The chatter and the cheer died down. Apparently no one had bothered to carry the lighting material.

'Why don't we ask the security guards?' someone suggested.

'I'll do it,' said Prem Arora and he sauntered off towards the guards. 'Guard sahib, do you have a matchbox?' he asked the Veerappan type, who only stroked his moustache in response. The other guard was more amicable and probably smarter too. He produced a matchbox from his trousers and handed it over to Prem, obviously to put a quick end to the tamasha.

Prem succeeded in putting the effigy on fire in the third

attempt. A loud roar almost brought the pump-house down. Frenzied dancing began.

'*De de pyaar de, pyaar de pyaar de re...*' started by Prem was picked up by the baraat.

The frustoos on the roof of the pump-house had enough stock of beer with them and were gradually and steadily getting drunk. The cool winter night, the hot hostel girls and the chilled beer flowing rapidly down the throat and seeping swiftly into the brain made a superman out of each one of them.

Only Rajveer Tomar was feeling like a Spiderman. He was usually the odd man out. Tomar, a junior final student from Bhind, always found the residents of Bhopla a bit too soft for his liking. According to him, if you don't flex your biceps every two minutes and swear at someone's mother or sister every four minutes, you aren't man enough.

Tomar was jumping around, ramming his thick shoulders into boys coming in his way, in what appeared to be a war dance from the hinterland of Bhind–Morena, once dacoit territory. Some of the boys who had been shoved around by Tomar in his drunken dancing tried to get even with him.

'Boss, if you jump down from the roof, the girls watching from the hostel would be highly impressed.' Ghanshyam Prasad planted a radical idea in Tomar's thas mind.

'Do you really think so?' Tomar grabbed Ghanshyam by his shoulders.

'Yes boss, they will start liking you from within.' Ghanshyam flailed his limbs, trying to escape.

Tomar suddenly released Ghanshyam and leapt down from the roof of the pump-house on the ground below. His right foot landed on a stone and there was a sickening crunch—his heel was fractured. Tomar was holding his ankle and cursed loudly at those looking down from the roof of the pump-house and grinning.

The eventuality of something like this happening to Tomar was always on the cards. He learnt the hard way that if, instead of using your two cerebral hemispheres you utilize your two testicles for thinking, you are bound to land in trouble some time.

Somehow, the news reached the girls. Initially they laughed, but later some of them did send messages of condolence. This created a lot of heartburn among the FOSLA members, most of whom started to plan their jumps on the next Valentine's Day.

After the jumping fiasco. Tomar was always called 'Langad', the lame one, until he passed out of the college.

⊕

On the fourteenth evening, JD was sitting inside Radhe tea stall opposite the college gate since 4.30. There were two reasons for his reaching early. One, he had nothing better to do than wait for Mansi and contemplate over a cup of hot tea the possibilities of a steaming kiss. Two, he knew it was better to play safe where girls are concerned—this highly unpredictable breed is prone to fly into a murderous rage if you are late even by a fraction of a second.

At 5.10, the royalty arrived. Mansi was wearing a white embroidered top over a pair of nicely fitting black linen pants. JD kept looking at her, forgetting for the moment that she was waiting for him. As always, Mansi looked stunning. With a face and figure as easy on the eye as hers, she complemented the clothes she wore and not vice versa. Recovering from his torpor, JD picked up his helmet and rushed out of the tea stall. He plonked the helmet over his head and started the bike. Mansi saw him coming and flashed a heart-busting smile. JD braked the bike smartly in front of Mansi, making the rear wheel go up in the air. Mansi slid behind him smoothly and they were off on their rendezvous.

'I can't resist saying you are looking good enough to eat,' said JD, turning back.

'I wouldn't have come with you if I had known you had cannibal tendencies,' teased Mansi.

'In case you have forgotten, we are going to Domino's to eat,' JD said.

'I know, I know!' Mansi tried to pacify JD. 'Tell me why you are wearing this helmet,' she tapped the back of JD's helmet with her knuckles.

'Why do you ask?'

'Just curious!'

'Try to make an intelligent guess,' JD smiled inside his helmet.

'Didn't I tell you I am not good at guessing games?'

'Well, it's for protection. Not in the conventional sense, but against prying eyes.'

'What do you mean?' Mansi asked.

'If anyone sees us, he will only see you riding pillion on the bike. You can always say that it was the brother of any one of your several class friends. And that you were going to her place for a birthday party.'

'So, wily Mr JD has thought of every little detail and I thought you were immersed in studies all the time.'

'Meet me more often and you will know more about me,' laughed JD.

Mansi didn't say anything, avoiding the topic. Soon they reached Domino's and JD parked his bike with a flourish right in front of the entrance. Getting down, he thrust his chest out and tightened his biceps. You can do that, especially when all the boys sitting outside on their bikes are drooling over your maal, an attractive catch such as Mansi. They entered the joint and went towards the service counter.

'I'll have a small pepperoni cheese pizza,' declared JD standing at the counter. 'What about you?'

'A fussili pasta in white sauce for me,' said Mansi, standing close behind JD.

'That'll be ₹249, sir. ₹99 for the pizza and ₹150 for the pasta,' said the smart young man at the till.

Before Mansi could react, JD handed over ₹250 to the young man. He took the one-rupee coin back and showed it to Mansi. 'We will use it for a toss later. If it's heads, we go for a spin on the "thandi sadak", if it's tails...'

'We head back to the hostel,' completed Mansi. 'Why did you pay? It was supposed to be my turn,' she complained.

'I can't anger St Valentine on this day,' grinned JD. 'Don't worry, you can pay on the next two dates.'

'An excellent technique to take a girl on repeated dates, Mr JD,' commented Mansi sarcastically.

JD kept smiling without saying anything. For him, Mansi's presence was reason enough to smile and feel happy. Love is like that! It enthralls, enraptures and enriches your life.

'Your order, sir,' said the young man, placing the tray laden with their food on the counter. JD picked up the tray and they sat down at a vacant table for two.

'I didn't see you in that wild, mad crowd dancing in front of the girls' hostel yesterday night, how come?' asked Mansi.

'Mehul and I were there but we didn't participate in the antics of Prem Arora and his gang. We remained in the background for some time, then came back to the hostel,' replied JD.

'It was quite funny, actually,' said Mansi, spooning off her pasta with gusto.

'Such scenes are routine in the boys' hostel. First, the guys will drink for any rhyme or reason...'

'Like...?' interrupted Mansi.

'Oh, it could be anything. Interns getting their first pay, winning a match, winning a bet, during Musical Night, the list is endless.'

'Then what happens?'

'Non-veg jokes are told, some iconic, some new. Raunchy numbers are played at full volume and finally the dancing begins. Believe me, the scene is more dangerous than what you witnessed yesterday,' JD informed.

Mansi started to laugh. 'You guys are really living it up. Life is quite sedate, almost boring, in the girls' hostel.'

'We can perk it up, just let us know. The entire boys' hostel is at your service,' JD offered with a straight face.

Mansi pointed her fork at JD threateningly. He put his hands up in mock surrender. Then both started to laugh, much to the delight and amusement of onlookers. JD was not bothered but Mansi was.

'Finish your pizza quickly so that we can leave,' she said, forking in the last of the remains of her pasta.

'Okay, but let's first toss to decide where we are going,' said JD, taking a large bite from the pizza.

'You can enact that stunt outside.' Mansi appeared a bit tense.

'No problem,' replied JD merrily, failing to catch Mansi's mood.

Coming out of Domino's, JD tossed the coin high and caught it in mid-air. 'Check out whether it's heads or tails,' he said, opening his fist in front of Mansi.

'It's heads,' said Mansi, after carefully examining the coin.

'Off we go on a ride to "thandi sadak,"' JD smiled victoriously.

'Thandi sadak' was an isolated stretch of road going uphill towards a government warehousing complex, which remained deserted after six in the evenings and was a favoured destination for lovelorn couples. JD started the bike and Mansi parked herself behind him. Soon they left the hustle and bustle of the market area behind and reached the relatively quiet residential area of the city. JD took a left from the Shivaji Square and reached the 'thandi sadak'. He put his bike in a lower gear as the engine required more power to go uphill. He stopped the bike near a clump of tall eucalyptus trees at the top of the hill. All the city lights were visible from this vantage point. The denizens of Bhopla called it 'the million-dollar view'.

'Oh, it's beautiful!' exclaimed Mansi, looking at the twinkling lights in the distance.

'Yes, the city looks extremely captivating from this point.' JD removed the helmet from his head and hung it from the handle. He switched off the ignition but both he and Mansi remained seated on the bike. It was quite apparent that they didn't intend to stay long.

'Have you come here before?' Mansi asked.

'On a few occasions, though not recently.'

'With whom?'

JD felt he could detect a faint trace of jealousy. It gave a nice little boost to his male ego. He smiled secretively, but said, 'Of course, with the gang. I remember the last time we were here it was Manish's birthday and we had quite a binge.'

Just then there was a sudden power failure and the entire city plunged into darkness. Even the moon was lost in the arms of dark clouds. The breeze suddenly picked up and it became quite chilly on the hilltop. The rustle of the eucalyptus leaves and chirping of the crickets added mystique to the night.

'It's so romantic, let me hug you,' JD looked back over his shoulder and stretched his arms towards her.

'I didn't know you had such powerful connections. The city lights have been switched off, the moon has disappeared and the crickets are singing their hearts out. I can't stop you, JD. I don't want to.' Mansi leaned towards JD and they went into a bone-crunching, heart-crushing, breath-stopping embrace that lasted and lasted and...

Suddenly, there was a sound of moving feet on the gravel and two ruffians appeared out of the dark. They moved towards the bike in quick measured steps and stood at the front and rear, blocking any escape.

One of them came up and grabbed the bike's handle. 'What's going on here?' he snarled.

'Having fun with the girl?' added the second, standing at the rear.

JD contemplated for a brief moment before deciding on his response. Then in a flash, he removed the helmet from the bike's handle and delivered a swinging blow on the face of the man standing in front. The man fell to the ground, bleeding profusely from his broken nose.

'Mansi, don't be afraid, just hold me tight,' shouted JD, starting the bike. He engaged the gear and twisted the accelerator to the max. The Hero Honda Splendor NXG shot off like an arrow. The man standing at the rear was caught unawares. He lunged forward and tried to grab Mansi but could only grasp the hand-rest just above the tail-light. He was dragged for some distance and then he let go, cursing loudly.

JD drove fast initially, but then eased the accelerator. The cool air had calmed his jarred nerves. He was basically a cool guy unruffled by most things, but the unexpected assault had unsettled him. Now regaining his composure, he started to hum under his breath.

'You really are too much,' commented Mansi, smiling pleasantly. 'We just escaped what could have been serious trouble and you are singing a song.'

JD didn't reply but started to sing loudly, *'Jindagi ek safar hai suhana, yahan kal kya ho kisne jana.'*

Mansi joined in and soon they reached the college campus. JD stopped the bike just ahead of the girls' hostel and Mansi got down.

'Hey, I am really sorry,' said JD with feeling.

'It was not your fault, so don't feel sorry. Such things happen in life. Smart people use them as learning experiences and don't repeat the same mistakes.' Mansi started to walk towards the hostel gate then stopped. She came back and kissed JD lightly on the cheek, 'Thanks for everything, JD.' She turned back again and went inside the hostel.

That night, sleep deserted JD as he tossed and turned in his bed. Suddenly his mobile beeped. Mansi had messaged him, 'You are cool and courageous. JD, you rock!'

Finally, sleep overtook JD until he was in another world, planning another tryst with his destiny, aka, Mansi.

16

Let's Keep Our Feelings on Hold

The pressure of the impending second professional exams was building up gradually. Instead of utilizing their time in multiplexes and malls learning newer filmi dance steps and the latest techniques of 'bird'watching, the students were now spending more time in and around the library. The girls had started paying less attention to their wardrobe and appearance, and the boys had begun to smell of unwashed armpits. But everybody looked sleep-deprived and fatigued. The exam phobia had started to take its toll on everybody.

JD and Mehul were seated in an alcove created by the almirahs containing medical tomes. They were trying to come to terms with 'inflammation', one of the most confusing chapters in Robbin's *Textbook of Pathology*. Manish and Lazarus, sitting opposite them, were trying to memorize the newer anti-emetic drugs from the textbook of pharmacology with every intention of vomiting them out during the exams and conveniently forgetting all about them.

Junaid had left the library after thirty minutes of intense study to get some fresh air and stale samosas. He had successfully ghotoed the differences between antemortem and postmortem hanging from J. P. Modi's *Textbook of Medical Jurisprudence and Toxicology*. This is of extreme importance in differentiating between a case of suicide and murder, when a body is found hanging.

'Cum out u losers samosas r wating,' Junaid sent an SMS to Mehul. He was standing in the corridor just outside the library. No food articles were allowed inside the library and the librarian, M. K. Mozumdar, was a stickler for rules.

Munching on their samosas, after they came out from the library, the gang discussed the strategy to prepare for the forthcoming exams. Everyone was especially worried about the pathology practical, and the horror stories associated with it.

'Do you know why during the last exams both Riyaaz Mamu and Danav flunked pathology?' Junaid asked.

'Tell us,' Manish stuffed the remaining samosa in his mouth.

'They had a *setting* with a lab technician who passed them the slips containing the diagnosis of the histopathology slides allotted to them.' Junaid inserted his hand inside the paper bag and took out another samosa. He was a samosa fanatic and could easily polish off seven to eight at a go.

'So, what was the problem?' Manish wanted to know.

'The technician passed them the slips all right but Dr T. R. Wasule switched the slides.'

'Then…'

'Then what! Riyaaz Mamu got the slides of the spleen and lungs but he had the slip mentioning the kidney and liver.'

'Shit…'

'And Danav was allotted the slides of the kidney and liver but his slip said the spleen and lungs.'

'Shit, man, shit…' Manish's disappointment was as real as if the tragedy had happened to him.

'Don't say shit again and again because shit can seal your fate,' Junaid's hand was reaching for yet another samosa in the bag.

'What do you mean shit can seal our fate?' Manish asked.

'Don't you remember? During the microbiology practical class you were allotted an excreta sample, which you examined under the microscope, demonstrating the ova and cysts of various intestinal parasites in it?' JD was a bit surprised.

'You mean those were real shit samples collected from guys harbouring roundworms, tapeworms and pinworms and preserved in the department of microbiology? *They* were given to us to locate the ova and cysts?' Manish appeared a bit shocked.

'You are behaving as if Dr K. P. Garg, HOD of microbiology, had thrown you in a septic tank and asked you to search for the ova of various worms,' JD said, a bit irritated. 'You will again be asked to examine the shit sample in the final exams and if you fail to show the ova and cysts in it, you'll be in deep shit.'

'Okay guys, let's not waste our time discussing shit when we don't even have the time to do it,' Junaid thought he had cracked a great joke.

'All this talk has reminded me of a joke,' smiled Lazarus. He had an encyclopaedic knowledge of dirty jokes and anything to do with human excreta or the bowel function immediately fired his imagination.

'I am all ears,' said Junaid.

Lazarus repeated one of his favourite non-veg jokes. Although Junaid had heard it several times he started to guffaw loudly. The rest were not amused.

'Oh, come on yaar. When will you get over your fixation with the human excreta?' JD turned and started to walk towards the lift.

'What about combined study during the night?' Junaid called out from the rear. 'At my place. With…Ammi's mutton rogan josh and biryani,' he dangled the bait.

JD turned back and embraced Junaid. 'Any time yaar, any time…' The other members of the gang hugged the duo from all sides.

⊕

The combined study session lasted from 8 p.m. to 2 a.m. with a half-hour rogan josh-biryani break, after which the gang dispersed. They decided to hold these sessions twice a week and help each other prepare for the exams. Everyone looked up to JD for guidance in pathology and pharmacology. Mehul was the master of microbiology and provided them with the extensive notes that he had prepared throughout the year.

Junaid generally lagged behind the others in all the three subjects but was way ahead of them in forensic medicine. This was a subject that fascinated him, because he was a conscientious reader of detective novels. He took delight in the realization that he now knew how to distinguish human blood from an animal's, compare bullet wounds and differentiate murder from suicide. The assistant professor who taught the subject, Dr R. P. Singh, was a tall, muscular guy with coarse features and a bushy moustache. His picture appeared fairly regularly in the newspapers, inspecting the scene of all major crimes in the city of Bhopla. If you didn't know him personally you could quite easily confuse him for the perpetrator rather than the investigator. His favourite lecture topics were common methods of committing suicide, illegal abortion, homicide and rape.

One night, JD and Mehul returned a bit early to their room on JD's bike. The heat and humidity was insufferable and the old fan in the room was itself gasping for breath. Mehul stripped to his dark blue VIP undies and lay down on the bed; within minutes he was fast asleep. JD opened the lone window of the room to reduce the stuffiness inside and sat down on the bed. He was finding it difficult to go off to sleep. He took out his mobile phone and navigated to the message inbox.

Mansi's terse one-liner was sitting at the top, 'Let's keep our feelings on hold till after the exams.' He read it for the hundredth time and smiled wistfully. He had sent an SMS the previous night asking 'Can we go out for dinner again?' The answer had left him a bit disappointed, but the reply was more or less on the expected lines. And yes, she had not refused! It was a sensible thing to do and JD knew it. If you are aiming for the top, no distraction is the golden rule. Yes, they would have to keep their feelings on hold.

Since that last meeting, they had not been able to spend time together alone. Sitting near each other in the classroom, meeting during the breaks or going to the canteen with the group didn't amount to being together in the real sense. JD longed to touch Mansi again. He could still feel the dampness of her palms, the warmth of her breath, the squeeze of her fingers and the fire on her lips. He felt a sharp pain shoot through his heart. That moment when they first held hands would remain etched in JD's memory forever. He knew he would never forget that first touch ever.

Sleep finally released him from his pained, perturbed state and embraced him in its tender arms. But then dreams took over and threw him straight back into the furnace of longing and desire.

⊕

The theory papers started amidst an atmosphere of foreboding and trepidation, but ended with hope and happiness. A Chinese proverb says: 'Keep a green tree in your heart, the singing bird will surely come.' The students seemed to be following the Chinese saying. Most of the students had done reasonably well and were starting to feel confident of getting thorough to the final professional.

The pharmacology practical went like a breeze. JD's gang was not overly worried about the forensic medicine practical. With Professor Junaid Ansari taking full charge, not only of guiding them about which topics to memorize, but also by making a *setting* to give them an idea beforehand of the twenty odd spotting specimens going to be put up during the practical exam. All he had to do was arrange a khamba of Royal Stag whisky, a favourite of Dr Shamsher Singh Pande, demonstrator in the department of forensic medicine responsible for arranging the specimens on the day of the exam.

The microbiology and pathology practical exam proved to be a different ball game altogether. In micro, the shit literally flew thick and fast. Most students were unable to demonstrate ova and cysts in the stool samples allotted to them. They became so nervous and shaky that when they were given Gram's stain and asked to stain the slides to delineate the bacteria, they ended up staining their faces, hands and aprons.

The pathology practical was an absolute massacre. The external examiner, Dr Nandini Sarabhai, was a six-feet-tall lady with a crisp manner and a crisper cotton sari tied six inches above the ankles. She was an old hand at conducting exams and knew all the tricks of the 'practical exam' trade. She was fully aware of the unholy nexus that existed between the demonstrators in the department and the students, by virtue of which most of them came to know the diagnosis of the histo-pathology slides allotted to them. Many students also knew beforehand about the gross specimens of various diseased organs kept for the viva voce.

To counter this, Dr Sarabhai had brought her own set of histo-pathology slides. Moreover, she rejected all the gross specimens selected prior to her arrival and chose the specimens afresh. To top it all, she refused to budge from the examination hall, not even going to the loo once.

It would be better not to describe the fate of the beleaguered students. The siege of the examination hall by Dr Sarabhai resulted in many students getting the slides all wrong. Boys looked harassed, the girls started to cry, with Minal Patnaik and Mita Varma leading the chorus. Dr T. C. Joshi, assistant professor and an honorary FOSLA member, got his chance to provide solace to the weeping womanhood. He patted the girls' backs soothingly, stroked their hair lovingly and wiped their tears with the cotton swabs available freely in the department. Dr T. C. Joshi was nicknamed 'Seetee' because whenever he narrowed his lips to say Joshi a shrill whistle emanated from his mouth. Whenever anyone called him 'Seetee' in his face, he corrected him with all seriousness, saying, 'It's TC not CT.'

The viva voce, the final step in the merciless torture of students, began in the afternoon. One student after another went in as if entering a torture chamber and came out looking asphyxiated and moribund. The specimen of the lung was diagnosed as the liver, the kidney was labelled as the spleen and the urinary bladder became the gall bladder.

After about an hour or so, the senior demonstrator called out, 'Junaid Ansari!'

'Good afternoon, madam. Good afternoon, sir,' Junaid entered the torture chamber and wished Dr Nandini Sarabhai and Dr T. R. Wasule in a trembling, barely audible voice. He had already heard the horror stories of the third-degree measures being used in the viva voce.

'What is the KW syndrome?' Dr Sarabhai launched a cruise missile.

'K…K…K…' Junaid was knocked down flat. He had not bothered to memorize the wretched syndrome.

'Forget it, tell me something about the Klinefelter's syndrome,' Dr Sarabhai released a short burst from her AK-47-like mouth.

'K…K…K…' Junaid started to stutter even more badly.

'Do you know what karyotyping is?' Dr Sarabhai took aim with her machinegun-like hands.

'K…K…K…' Junaid slumped back in his chair, gasping for breath.

'Yes, K…K…K…Kiran! Is that what you want to say? Instead of studying pathology you have been doing research on Shah Rukh Khan!' Dr Nandini Sarabhai was shaking with rage and her terrifying persona would have made even the fearsome wrestler, The Great Khali, scoot from the fighting ring.

'Okay now, take hold of yourself,' Dr Wasule consoled Junaid in an encouraging voice. 'Throw some light on this specimen,' he pointed towards a formalin-filled glass jar containing the liver of some unfortunate drunkard who must have died of liver cirrhosis.

Junaid had not yet fully recovered from the frontal attack launched by Dr Sarabhai and took some time to open his mouth. 'What?'

'Throw some light on this specimen,' Dr Wasule repeated his question menacingly.

Junaid looked at the glass jar standing in relative darkness on one side of the table. He got up from his chair and started to walk towards the door.

'Hey, where are you going? Your viva is not over yet!' shouted Dr Wasule.

Junaid kept moving away from them.

'Come back you fat, little K…K…K…Shah Rukh,' hollered Dr Sarabhai.

Junaid went towards the fridge kept near the door and lifted the emergency light standing on top of it. He brought it back, switched it on and aimed it on the specimen jar pointed to by Dr Wasule.

'Is it all right now, sir?' he asked innocently, trying to be of some help.

Dr Sarabhai and Dr Wasule almost fell off their seats, convulsing with laughter.

Most students would have failed, but for the involvement of Dr P. K. Saxena, HOD of biochemistry, who wanted his son Sumit to be passed. Dr Sarabhai, an inherently fair person, notwithstanding her fierce personality, decided to pass all the students who had done as badly as Sumit Saxena. That meant only a handful flunked the exam.

⊕

The results were not altogether unexpected. Mansi Manchanda topped with JD a close second. Surprisingly, Mehul Upulkar had moved up and was now in the top ten. To their utter disbelief and delight, the three musketeers Junaid, Lazarus and Manish successfully crossed the frontier, avoiding the landmines, evading the bullets and ducking the bombs of the enemy. Unfortunately, in spite of everybody's full sympathies, FOSLA King Bhavesh Mehta couldn't appear in the exams as his attendance was far too unsatisfactory, which meant that he would have to appear after six months along with the detained batch.

If JD was disappointed with the results, he didn't show it. Maybe it was his own shortcoming that he couldn't keep his feelings on hold as successfully as Mansi. Did that mean she was smarter or more mature? Either way it didn't matter to JD—he was head over heels in love with her.

17

Reverse FOSLA

Preparations for the annual carnival were in full swing. Love was in the air, FOSLA was on the move, and frustoos had a song on their lips. The atmosphere was electric and hopes soared high. The playground in front of the college building was being decked up for the grand night, which included a massive cleaning drive and painting of the rusted metal fence.

Clusters of students could be seen discussing what stalls to put up. Some girls and boys were very clear that they wanted to have no truck with the opposite sex and wanted to avoid dealing with them altogether. But there were many who didn't want to let go of this opportunity of togetherness.

A day prior to the carnival, mini-trucks and loading-autos started to arrive at the ground in the afternoon. They were loaded with tents, green carpeting, shamiyanas, tables, chairs, plastic tanks, tubs, fancy electric fixtures, spotlights, spools of electric wire, banners and buntings.

Early morning, on the day of the carnival, the entire area had been cordoned off, the green carpeting was laid out, the stalls were ready and the work force started to arrive. The students who had put up lucky dip and games stalls were busy decorating them. A stage was erected in the centre for the DJ who was there mainly to play song requests from the students. Most of the requests generally came from FOSLA members who dedicated their dil ka dard through Bollywood songs, voicing their heartbreak to their heroines. Unfortunately, unlike in the movies, the girls did not flutter their eyelashes rapidly, heave their bosoms provocatively or shake their buttocks tantalizingly. Instead, if anyone could hear their inner thoughts, they would hear plans to clobber these slobbering buffoons.

Two enterprising motorcycle dealers had put up stalls to entice the medicos doing their residencies. After all, they were earning between ₹15,000 to 20,000 in lieu of working their asses off the entire day in inhuman conditions! A Maruti true-value dealer had also put up a stall with some really cheap second-hand cars, mostly Maruti 800s, to try his luck with newly married residents. No new car dealer bothered to even put up a banner. Only the small Nano car had been advertised as khushion ki chhabi, because the dealer was smart enough to realize that it was all these broke doctors could dream of.

Some twenty-odd caterers had put up food stalls selling Chinese, Italian, South Indian, Punjabi, Mughlai (biryani, kebabs, keema samosa), Banarsi chaat (made in Bhopla), Tan-Tana-Tan ice-cream, cold drinks, sweets, popcorn, burf ka gola and candyfloss. All the caterers invariably spelt their professional services as 'Caters': Noori Caters, Baba Caters, Rajdhani Caters, etc.

Only non-alcoholic beverages were allowed inside the carnival. Booze was a total no-no! But that rule probably applied only to the staff members and, possibly, not even to all of them. As far as students were concerned, by 6 p.m. most had already started taking 'prophylaxis' against the dumb rule. The booster doses were cunningly smuggled inside the carnival venue in hipflasks or smaller 'quarter' packing.

JD, Mehul, Mansi and Minal had a lucky dip stall, the profits from which were to go to an orphanage. Lazarus, Junaid and Manish were drawing huge crowds in a nearby stall with open-flash, luring students who wanted to become billionaires in one night. Of course, the profits were to end in their pockets and were to be utilized during the weekend for a grand booze party at the Tentacles, a popular pub in the Hyper Mall.

Gestapo members Rajeev Gaur, Mannu Sharma and Shantanu Sikarwar were hanging around the open-flash stall, motivating suckers to try their luck. After all, they too had a stake in the profits and the party at the Tentacles. Suddenly the crowd at the stall erupted in loud cheering. Riyaaz Mamu, who had played his very first hand, got a trail of queens (although technically he could take in four as he was still unmarried). What no one knew was that he was also a part of the gambling cartel and was to receive a percentage of the loot. This increased the confidence level of the teeming masses who started to place bigger bets and lose greater amounts.

The DJ's voice rose above the din as he dedicated a song to Reshmi Khanna, from an unknown admirer. This was the usual tactic adopted by frustoos to provide solace to their bleeding hearts. And when the song is dedicated to the HOD of medicine's daughter, you need a cast-iron heart to let your name be known.

'Here it goes,' the DJ shouted with all his might. '"*Hame tumse pyaar kitna, ye ham nahi janate…*" lovely song for a lovely girl.' Kishore Kumar's mellifluous voice started playing.

'This is Prem Arora's song request! Don't you remember the bugger sang the same song during the musical night? *Marega saala…*' Riyaaz Mamu declared, biting on the keema samosa passed to him by Junaid. A disposable paper plate loaded with keema samosas was on the table right in front of Junaid, who was gobbling them up after sprinkling them liberally with green chutney, which probably had less coriander leaves and more green chillies and, of course, mixed with millions of amoeba, giardia, E. coli, salmonella and shigella.

'Hi friends!' Prem Arora arrived at the cards stall and greeted everybody in a voice that was already starting to slur under the influence of alcohol. He was with another ISO 9000 certified frustoo, Nandlal Nagar.

Mannu first looked to his left, then right, as if trying to locate who the friend Prem Arora was referring to was. Prem got the message but ignored the insult; he was in high spirits and nothing could spoil his mood.

'How are things, Nandlal?' Mannu inquired, replacing 'N' with 'L'.

'Okay, like.' Nandlal Nagar believed in moving with the times, especially with regard to the current lingo. His problem was his limited vocabulary. You take away okay, like, cool, anyways, fuck and chick and he would be left utterly speechless.

'I am feeling really thirsty,' Prem Arora winked at Mannu. He took out a quarter of Blender's Pride whisky and showed it to Mannu before slipping it back into his hip pocket.

'Same here,' Mannu warmed up to Prem's idea. 'Let's go get a two-litre Coke bottle from the cold drinks stall.

'I'll do it,' said Riyaaz Mamu. He was above suspicion, as everyone including the staff knew he was a teetotaler.

Senior staff members were on the prowl, lurking unobtrusively near the stalls, mingling with the students camouflaged in T-shirts, jeans and caps. Some even went to the extent of checking at the back of the stalls for any behind-the-scene booze parties.

Riyaaz Mamu brought the Coke bottle along with a stack of styrofoam glasses and kept them on a table inside the stall. He opened the bottle and poured Coke into some of the glasses and asked Junaid and Lazarus to take them to the nearby stall where JD, Mansi, Mehul and Minal were stationed.

Mannu and Prem Arora came inside the stall and looked at the half-empty Coke bottle with satisfaction. Prem took out his whisky quarter and poured it into the bottle.

'Do you guys also have some booze? A quarter of whisky won't do!' Prem looked at the group.

'Hold the bottle, Prem, while I add my half of gin,' said Mannu.

'I think I'll stiffen it a bit more with the rum I have got.' Rajeev Gaur transferred the contents of the hip flask he was carrying into the Coke bottle.

'That's it,' Prem Arora said with contentment, shaking the Coke bottle gently. 'One sip, and never a dull moment afterwards.'

'Nothing like a fizzy cocktail to have fun,' opined Mannu.

'Now! Let's taste the devil's brew.' Prem poured a little in one glass and gave it to Mannu.

'It's strong!' Mannu admitted, gulping.

'Hey, a bottle of Sprite is lying in the corner,' said Rajeev Gaur, pointing to it. 'Let's use it to dilute our mix.' So the Sprite was added to the Coke + whisky + gin + rum cocktail, and served.

'Odd sort of taste. I suppose that whisky was all right, Prem? You hadn't been fooled into buying desi tharra, had you?' Mannu stared at Prem doubtingly.

'Of course, it was all right. I bought it from Shivhare Wines. He knows we are regulars. He won't dare cheat us.' Prem was confident.

'Oh well, it must be the Sprite then. Anyway, cheers everyone,' said Mannu, knocking off the contents of his glass in one go.

'Cheers,' sang everyone merrily.

'What the fuck!' Danav Sisodia cursed, entering the stall. 'Who the fuck has stolen my Sprite bottle?'

'There is no need to get so upset over a half-empty bottle of Sprite,' Prem Arora tried to pacify Danav.

'It wasn't a half-empty bottle of Sprite, you fools! It was pure, undiluted Smirnoff vodka in the bottle.' Danav looked really pissed.

'My God! That will make the brew even more lethal!' exclaimed Rajeev.

'Even better!' lurched Prem, catching hold of Danav to steady himself.

'Here, have some, enjoy and don't behave like a chutia,' Mannu poured out some of the remaining brew in a fresh glass.

'Don't call me a chutia, you thieves.'

'Only a chutia will leave vodka lying like that in a place packed with boys,' countered Mannu.

'Yes, an unclaimed bottle of vodka is more unsafe than a bikini-clad girl in this stall,' Rajeev spoke philosophically. Rajeev didn't say that the girl was safe. She was also unsafe but less than the bottle of vodka. Probably because if you put your mouth on the vodka bottle, it won't shout like a girl. My, what sound thinking even when drunk!

'Okay, stop it,' Mannu commanded. 'Someone go get JD here before this phaadu cocktail is finished.'

'I'll fetch him, the poor fellow must be thirsss...ty,' slurred Prem and walked out. He saw Reshmi Khanna and her group of giggly girls pass by and instead of going towards JD's stall, started to follow them, panting like a dog on heat.

Reshmi stopped at Ragini Ratra's stall to play the dart game. Ragini was the exact opposite of Reshmi. She was short, thin, dark and bland. No curves, no chutzpah, no spice, in fact a totally non-spectacular specimen but for the spontaneous sweetness that flowed from her like a pure, clear mountain stream.

The game was pretty straightforward. You were given four darts for ₹20 and for each dart hitting the bull's eye you got a small Bar-One worth ₹5. So there was no chance of Ragini losing money even if you hit the bull's eye with all four darts. Most people couldn't find the target even once and all the money remained with Ragini.

Reshmi and her group moved on after a few unsuccessful attempts but Prem Arora got stuck at the stall, where he spent most of his inebriated evening.

The group at the cards stall was getting restless. 'Where the fuck has Prem Arora gone?' Whenever Mannu got high he stopped using bhencho and shifted to fuck. If he started to use the F-word it was a sure sign that he was drunk, you didn't need a breath-analyser to confirm it.

In his senses, Mannu stuck religiously to bhencho, in keeping with the colourful language used by today's youth. According to him, bhencho was the most versatile word available in the entire universe and he used it like punctuation. 'Why don't you go and fetch your friend JD,' Mannu ordered Junaid, who was now sitting idle as most of the gamblers had gone broke.

'No problem,' said Junaid, leaving the stall. He returned shortly with JD and Riyaaz Mamu by his side.

Mannu perked up on seeing JD, he was in really high spirits. Picking up the Coke bottle he brought it near JD's mouth. JD had taken a prophylactic dose of whisky around 5 p.m. and a booster dose at 7 and was himself quite cheerful.

'JD, JD,' sang Mannu.

'Yes, Mannu,' responded JD.

'Want daaru?'

'No, Mannu.'

''Telling lies.'

'Yes, Mannu.'

'Open your mouth.'

There was no Ha, ha, ha! Only glug, glug, glug…as JD belted down the remains of the Coke bottle pushed into his mouth by Mannu.

Junaid, Lazarus and Manish went off to bring biryani and kebabs. Mannu, Rajeev, Shantanu and JD kept sitting in the stall, floating in a mist of whisky, gin, rum and vodka. Riyaaz Mamu sat at a distance, keeping a close watch on their deteriorating state of consciousness, his face grim with worry.

'Ha, ha, ha…' Mannu started to laugh in a staccato manner, not much different from the starting sound of an old diesel generator set. JD, Rajeev and Shantanu all joined in but petered out soon. Mannu went on and on gathering momentum by the minute. Riyaaz Mamu got up from his seat to switch him off. Mannu leaned back in his chair and started to laugh so loudly that Riyaaz Mamu could see his uvula (the small finger-like structure hanging from the palate) waggling at the back of his throat. The gusts of four kinds of alcohol intermingled with each other hit Riyaaz Mamu directly in his face. He rushed back and sat down, fearing that he, too, would get intoxicated, so strong was the stench.

Junaid and his team returned with biryani, kebabs, rumali roti and rasgullas. The food was laid on the table and the feast began.

'Hey, Prem Arora is coming in this direction and he seems to be in a terrible rush,' Junaid informed the others.

'Where the fuck was he all this while?' slurred Mannu.

'Something terrible has happened!' Prem Arora slumped in an empty chair beside Mannu. 'You have got to help me!' His pink complexion had turned ashen black.

Mannu tried to concentrate. 'What is the problem?' he asked, placing his head on Prem Arora's shoulder.

'You know Ragini Ratra? The short, dark intern, the one at the dart game stall?'

'Umm.'

'Open your eyes, please don't go to sleep for God's sake!' pleaded Prem.

'I am listening, go aaannn…' Mannu jerked open his eyes.

'I was at her stall the entire evening.'

'You bastard…that's where you were.'

Prem didn't react to the abuse, he was in dire straits. 'We talked about a lot of things. I was enjoying her company and you know I was brimming with whisky, rum, gin…and what not.'

'So you kissed her and she threatened to report the matter to the dean?' Mannu gave a lecherous smile.

'Nothing of that sort happened. How can you do it with so many people around?' (Meaning, you can do it when no one is around.) Prem's voice became shrill with urgency.

'So, bhencho, why don't you tell us in plain and simple words what happened instead of talking in circles? My head is already spinning like a lattoo.' Mannu was sobering down fast. He had already come back to his normal B-word. The F-word had not been used for some time.

'I was so high, so bloody fucking high that before I knew what I was doing, I proposed to her.' Prem was literally in tears.

Mannu jerked up and sat bolt upright in his chair. He tried to clear the alcoholic mist that surrounded his brain. 'Did she accept?' he asked, with a big yawn, displaying his uvula again and sending a gust of lethal fumes in the atmosphere that must have killed thousands of bacteria and viruses.

'Accept! She jumped up with joy, held my hands ever so tightly, looked deep into my eyes and said "Yes! Please, yes!"'

'*Ab kya hoga?*' Mannu's voice quivered.

'You're doomed,' Rajeev was the epitome of sorrow.

'I don't know what's going to happen. All I know is that it is a grave situation. I am in serious trouble,' Prem choked and could speak no further.

'Perhaps she will not take it seriously and forget all about it by the morning,' Riyaaz Mamu suggested hopefully.

'Not a chance, Riyaaz Mamu! You were not there to see her expression, her joy, she has taken it in all seriousness. She won't forget it by the morning, not a chance. I am sure by morning it'll be a case of "Guess what, girls! Prem Arora proposed to me and we are going to be married as soon as I finish my internship!" Oh God, oh God!' Prem clasped his head. 'Everyone, right down to the sweepers in NMC, will come to know that Prem Arora and Ragini Ratra are engaged by nine o'clock tomorrow.'

'I presume you are not keen on the idea of marrying her?' Riyaaz Mamu asked.

'Me marrying her! Can't you see? I—a tall, fair, handsome Punjabi lad marrying a short, dark nondescript girl like Ragini? I just have to say yes for marriage and my mom will get me a Sonam Kapoor look-alike in no time.'

Riyaaz Mamu nodded his head understandingly and looked carefully at Prem. Indeed, he was tall and fair but only people who liked Virendra Sehwag would call him handsome, and he had already lost more hair than the cricketer. Moreover, unlike Sehwag there was hardly any chance of him earning enough money in the near future to get a hair transplant.

'This needs some thought,' Riyaaz Mamu finally agreed.

'Thank you, Riyaaz Mamu, thank you!'

'Surely there must be something you can do… Can't you go back and explain it was all in fun?' Rajeev Gaur tried to be of help.

Prem Arora gave a contemptuous laugh. 'You go and explain,' he said.

Riyaaz Mamu raised his hand. 'It's tricky. I see your point, Prem. Let's think in silence.'

After about ten minutes, Riyaaz Mamu suddenly got up from his chair and started to pull at his lower lip, a sure sign that he was deep in thought. Before he could tear away the lower lip from his mouth he sat down again. 'I think I've got the answer,' Riyaaz Mamu smiled with satisfaction.

'What is it, please tell me,' begged Prem.

Riyaaz Mamu paused for effect. 'Go around the carnival and propose to as many girls as you can catch hold of before the night ends.'

⊕

The next morning, Dr V. K. Jain, vice dean and in-charge of the carnival committee, was horrified to find forty-five empty bottles of various brands of whisky, rum and gin lying behind the stalls. But the sweepers were delighted, they made a neat sum out of the bottle sale and bought a full bottle of hooch for their very own carnival!

18

Feelings Let Loose

It took JD the whole of the next day to wash out the lethal brew from his system. Isolated pieces of conversation with Mansi came back to him in flashes, like fragments of a dream. He kept playing and replaying them in his still foggy mind...

'Red suits you,' he had said when he first set eyes on her. Mansi was looking stunning in a bright red T-shirt and black jeans.

'Someone is looking handsome himself,' she teased him. 'You are looking quite a dude in all black and I like your gelled look.'

'I follow you,' he said. 'Your dress sense, I mean. Last time you were all in black so here I am dressed up like you, but you have switched to red and black.'

'Thank you. I get the message.' Girls would make great radio stations, they have good transmitters and even better receivers, he thought.

'You captivate me,' he said, drawing in a deep breath.

Mansi flashed her million-dollar smile. It killed JD instantly.

Mehul and Minal had left the stall for some time. He didn't remember exactly for what, probably to get something to drink or eat or maybe both.

'When do we meet again? It's been so long,' he had said, coming to stand near her. The sides of their bodies touched and electric sparks flew.

'Whenever you want,' she replied non-committally.

'There is no need to keep our feelings on hold?' he grinned.

'I think so,' she smiled but didn't look him in the eyes.

'I'll pick you up from the turn just beyond the hostel gate tomorrow at 7 p.m.'

⊕

'Bloody hell!' JD jumped out of bed. It was almost 7 p.m. and he had neither shaved nor taken a bath. If not Michael Schumacher then at least Narain Karthikeyan must have been impressed by the speed with which JD got ready. He was at the meeting point near the hostel on the dot at 7 p.m. Mansi arrived after a few moments.

JD had deliberately chosen to wear a red T-shirt with black jeans. The T-shirt had very short sleeves and his toned, rippling biceps were prominently on display. Mansi was all in black. For a while they looked at each other in amusement then JD started to laugh, pointing a finger at Mansi and she began to chuckle mirthfully, tugging at his red T-shirt. This set the tone for a happy, carefree evening of togetherness.

'What's the plan like?' Mansi straddled the pillion seat of JD's bike.

'Depends on how much time you have.'

'I have to get back latest by 10.'

'That means we can catch a movie, but then you will have to miss dinner.'

'So...tell me.'

'Wait, let me start the bike, I seem to think better on the wheels. The throbbing engine and the rushing wind clears my mind.'

'I hope you are not still suffering from last night's hangover. Junaid told me what you guys drank in the carnival.'

'Even I didn't know the bastards had mixed whisky, rum,

gin and vodka, all in one bottle.' JD started the bike and cruised off smoothly.

'Why do you drink, JD?' Mansi asked sweetly in JD's ear.

'That's a tough one. I'll give you my reply after some time, first let us decide where we are going.'

'You decide, you think better on the wheels.'

'Let's go to the coffee shop of Corona Grand.'

'It's a five-star hotel, won't the prices be exorbitant?'

'Anything for you, precious.'

Mansi didn't react to the endearment used by JD. After a while she said, 'Don't you remember it's my turn to pay? The last two times we went out, you insisted upon paying. I am not carrying that kind of money.'

'We will just have coffee at Corona Grand and then later we can eat Chinese at Jai Santoshi Maa Restaurant.' JD appreciated the fact that unlike many other girls, Mansi believed in sharing expenses. He was relieved that the girl he was dating was not high-maintenance.

'Done.' Mansi clutched JD's shoulders as he accelerated the bike.

The coffee shop of Corona Grand was on the ground floor, overlooking the swimming pool. The brightly lit pool was abuzz with skimpily clad women and well-heeled hi-society folks from Bhopla's Page Three circuit. JD's attention was drawn towards a stout man in tight swimming trunks paying extra attention to a PYT (Pretty Young Thing). Two days later JD was surprised to see the man's photo along with his fat wife in the local newspaper, with a caption describing him as the richest man in Bhopla.

Mansi and JD selected a table near the large French windows with an uninterrupted view of the pool. After about five minutes, a waiter in a black suit, crisp white shirt and a red and black striped tie discreetly placed the leather-bound menu on the table and retreated quietly.

'I thought he was a guest coming to sit at the table next to us,' commented JD with a wry smile.

'Wear your attitude. Don't bother about your clothes is what the self-help gurus say,' Mansi tried to boost JD's confidence.

'But when the lower half of your attitude means jeans that have not been washed for a whole month, your attitude goes for a toss.'

JD opened the menu and started to read it in a reverse manner like Urdu, first the price then the description, which was pretty elaborate, and lastly the name of the item. He traced his finger down and up, and down again, finally stopping at 'Cappuccino', which at ₹150 a cup was the cheapest item on the list. Its description was so exhaustive that not only could customers learn to make good cappuccino, they could in fact go in for coffee cultivation in the hills of Coorg.

'This misadventure of drinking coffee in a five-star hotel is going to set us back by a cool three hundred bucks,' said JD in a hushed voice. 'Let's scoot from here.'

'I have that much with me. Once I've decided to come here, I am not going to run away even though I feel the whole thing to be outrageous,' Mansi said with finality.

'We could have had two bloody full dinner dates with that much money,' grumbled JD.

'Enjoy the AC, drool at the bikini-clad girls and soak in the ambience. It isn't such a bad deal, especially for you, JD. And I have not included the actual cost of the coffee in the list.'

JD waved at the waiter and placed the order. If the waiter felt vindicated in his assessment of their penury, he didn't let it show. He bowed courteously and went back graciously.

'I don't know if I'll be able to afford such places ever,' said

JD, focusing hard on a bombshell in a black, two-piece bikini.

'I have serious doubts about that. These places are for people loaded with money and for freeloaders like bureaucrats and politicians. Doctors don't belong here, they are supposed to be with ailing humanity,' the stinging sarcasm in Mansi's tone took JD by surprise.

'Fuc… Forget them. Let's talk about something else.'

'That reminds me, you were going to tell me why you drink,' Mansi leaned forward and fixed her gaze on JD.

All JD could concentrate on was her flawless complexion, chiselled features and ripe full lips painted red. He bent forward and before Mansi could react, planted a gentle kiss on her lips.

'I asked about your drinking habit, not your kissing addiction,' Mansi slumped back in her seat.

'Recommend me to the Bhatt camp. I'll prove to be a much better serial kisser than that ape they have in their movies.' JD laughed a bit more loudly than is permissible in the five-star setting.

'Don't try to sidetrack the issue. I know you are avoiding answering my question,' Mansi protested.

Before JD could answer, the waiter arrived with their coffee and with a lot of fuss placed the cups in front of JD and Mansi. He could well have been laying down a five-course meal. Certainly in that much time, the waiter at Jai Santoshi Maa restaurant would have served at least ten tables.

'I don't know myself why I drink,' JD revealed when the waiter departed. 'I had never given it a thought till you asked. As it is, I hardly drink. It is only during the parties or some celebration or some other such masti we are having in the hostel that I have alcohol.'

'Don't think that I am intruding upon your privacy, or pestering you, or trying to be preachy. I am just plain and simple curious. Some girls in the hostel also do have beer or gin occasionally,' Mansi lifted the cup and took a small dainty sip.

'Beer reminds me of my maternal uncle, who is about eight years older than me. He once offered me beer while I was in class twelve. It was so bitter I spit out the entire thing.'

'Yes I know, one of the seniors once pushed some down my throat and I literally gagged.' Mansi joined JD in giving her opinion on beer.

'With beer it is said that the first forty bottles are wasted. If you persist, then from the forty-first onwards, you start enjoying its bubbly, frothy bitterness and then you are hooked for life,' JD sermonized like an expert.

'So which bottle are you on at the moment? Have you already crossed the barrier of forty and are hooked to it?' Mansi took a bigger sip this time.

'No, no, nothing of the sort. In fact, I want to get hooked on to something else, but the person is not taking the bait.' JD picked up his cup and took a large satisfying slurp.

'How subtle you boys are,' Mansi smiled mischievously.

All of a sudden the conversation died down. They sat looking out of the window at people frolicking in the pool. The tall eucalyptus trees in the distance swayed gently in the late evening breeze. The moon had not yet bothered to make an appearance.

JD took a deep breath. He was prepared to sit like this till eternity. Mansi's presence affected him in so many ways—it calmed him, excited him, made him happy and anxious, all at the same time. Her nearness stoked his desires, leaving him hanging between longing and belonging. He was absolutely sure Mansi was the girl he wanted to spend his entire life with.

'What are you thinking?' Mansi broke his reverie.

'About us. About you. Mainly you.'

'Can I be a part of your thoughts, especially about me?'

'Why, sure. You know, Mansi, you are a multidimensional person. There are so many dimensions to your persona that I keep discovering something new about you every time we meet.' JD paused and looked deep in Mansi's beautiful eyes. 'What am I searching for?' he thought. 'Her feelings for me, whether she likes me, does she love me?' He only had questions, no answers.

'Hey, I have lost you again,' Mansi nudged him.

'The best thing I like about you is your thousand-watt smile. It killed me the first time I saw it and the effect has not worn out one bit,' JD kept searching for some clue in Mansi's eyes.

'Don't stop,' Mansi prodded him.

'You are the most beautiful girl in the world.'

'Don't stop.'

'You are the most graceful person I have ever met. You are intelligent, you are cool, you are tough, you are kind…'

'Stop, stop! Or I'll die of happiness. Most things you said may or may not be right. I don't know for myself. No one ever analysed me in such minute detail. But you missed out on one important aspect of my personality.'

'What is that? I thought I was spot on.' JD smiled at last.

'You know. JD, I am a very practical person. Very! All my decisions are usually well thought out. No knee-jerk reactions for me, because I don't believe in feeling sorry afterwards. Repenting is not a word in my dictionary.'

The waiter was hovering in the background for quite some time. He came up and placed the bill on their table, simultaneously taking away the empty cups.

Mansi swooped down and picked up the bill before JD could get it. 'A cool ₹340 with taxes for two cups of coffee.'

'I am sorry, it was my stupid idea.'

'But I am not. Thank you for your multidimensional theory. I'll happily pay ₹340 rupees for that kind of analysis any time.'

JD and Mansi came out of the coffee shop hand in hand and strolled towards the parking lot. On reaching his bike, JD released Mansi's hand and turned towards her. He raised his hands slowly and held Mansi's face tenderly in the cup of his palms, as if holding something very precious, very fragile. He raised her face up gradually and gazed lovingly in her almond-shaped eyes. Mansi met his gaze unflinchingly and they remained that way, frozen in time.

JD brought his face down and placed his lips gently over Mansi's. It appeared as if he was sucking nectar from the most beautiful flower on earth. Mansi's eyes closed and her lips parted on their own. The passion, the fire, the heat singed both their souls. JD kept holding Mansi's delicate face ever so tenderly. For him it was not a mere kiss, it was a prayer, a hope, a need that he wanted to imprint on Mansi's heart. Whenever she would think of this moment, she would feel his lips on hers.

On the way back, JD kept holding Mansi's hand tightly in his left hand while controlling the bike with his right. He felt at peace with himself, there was fragrance in the air and the night looked mysteriously beautiful.

'Say something,' he said, looking back over his shoulder.

'I don't know what to say.' Mansi's feelings were in a flux. She liked the way JD had held her face, so tenderly, so lovingly, but she didn't really know what to make of it. She was still confused, even overawed by the events of the evening. She was probably disturbed because she had let her feelings loose, she had lost control and she liked to be in control. Always.

'Want to eat Chinese food?' asked JD, releasing her hand. The traffic had become thick and he needed to control the bike with both hands.

'I don't feel like it any more. Please drop me at the hostel.'

'Is something wrong?'

'Why should there be? It's just that I am not in the mood for it.'

'Okay,' said JD, a little perturbed. Was something amiss? Was Mansi hurt in some way? He was clueless, and that left a hollowness in him, which gnawed at his heart.

Mansi got down from the bike near the hostel gate and smiled sweetly at JD. 'Thanks for a wonderful evening.'

'The reverse is more true. After all, you picked the tab.'

'Think nothing of it. It was small change paid for getting my psychoanalysis done by an emerging shrink,' Mansi laughed her tinkling laugh, putting in shade the twinkling stars. Her glowing face made the moon duck behind the clouds and in the ensuing darkness, JD, serial kisser par excellence, planted a quick kiss on her lips and took off on his Splendor NXG.

19

Visit to Nahakganj Hospital

'Where were you the entire evening?' Mehul quizzed JD the moment he entered the room.

'Generally.'

'Don't give me that crap, tell me the truth.'

'My bike was giving trouble so I had to take it to the mechanic.'

'Bullshit!'

'My, my, for someone born and brought up in Dhond you seem to have picked up quite a smattering of American expletives,' JD spoke acidly.

'I won't be cowed down by your public-school English. It's for your own good that I am being so obstinate. Now will you tell me, or do you want me to tell you who you were with?' Mehul was getting agitated.

'Tell me, Mr Sherlock Holmes,' acid flowed from JD's tongue.

'You were with Mansi.'

'So, I was with Mansi. How does it matter to you or to anyone else?'

'I don't know about others but it does matter to me. You are my friend and I can't see you jeopardizing your career for a girl.'

'But I am doing nothing of that sort,' JD mellowed down immediately.

'You may not agree but you are doing exactly that. Did you ever sit down and analyse why you didn't top in the second professional? Why you ended up being second best? With your kind of brains, the number-one slot should be yours for the taking.'

JD sat down quietly. He seemed to have lost the will to fight back. Mehul had hit the nail on its head and there was not much JD could do about it. How could he tell him that you can't enter or delete emotions at will, it is not in your hands. Your heart doesn't operate like a computer.

Mehul sat down opposite JD. 'You did not come to college today, and I know the reason why, so you don't have to tell another lie.' Without mentioning it, Mehul had pointed out that JD was nursing a hangover from the drinking binge he had during the carnival night. 'Next Friday, our batch is going for a two-day field visit to the Primary Health Centre (PHC), Nahakganj. It is part of the curriculum and Professor P. P. Dwivedi has made it mandatory for everyone to attend.'

'Where is this god-forsaken place? I have never heard of it.'

'Don't talk like that, who knows, you might get posted there after postgraduation.'

'No way!' JD dismissed the idea altogether.

'Don't bet on it. Haven't you heard of the government bond which makes it mandatory for doctors to put in a minimum of one year of rural service after completing their degree?'

'Why don't they send guys from IIT, IIM and NLIU to improve the lot of villagers? Why only doctors?' he said, referring to the Indian Institutes of Technology, the Indian Institutes of Management and the National Law Institute University.

'Because ours is a noble profession.' Even Mehul couldn't hide the sarcasm in his voice.

'So keep screwing doctors in the name of their profession. Pay them peanuts, post them in hellholes with zero infrastructure, provide them absolutely no facilities and yet expect them to perform miracles.'

'Cool down, yaar, no one is asking you to stay in a village,' Mehul said light-heartedly.

'I have no problem with going to a village,' JD flared up. 'What I want these bastards to understand is that sending a doctor to a remote village will not resolve the hardships faced by the villagers. They also need electricity, roads, safe drinking water and proper sewage disposal. How long will 75 per cent of the population of this mahaan country keep defecating in the open fields, on railway tracks and by the side of the highways.'

'I fully agree with what you are saying. The problem is of political treachery and bureaucratic apathy.'

'Don't forget corruption! Rajiv Gandhi said that the rupee shrinks down to fifteen paise by the time it reaches the actual beneficiary.'

'That was in the good old times, now not a single paisa reaches the people,' Mehul remarked.

'Hey guys! Have you had dinner?' Bhavesh Mehta peeped in. 'They have chhola-bhatura and kheer in the mess today.' Compared to the routine offering of watery potato curry, burnt vegetables, leathery chapatis and gooey rice, this was a meal for kings.

'No,' said Mehul, looking at his watch. 'It's almost ten o'clock. I hope the mess guys have not closed shop.'

'They stay open till 10, but we will have to rush,' said Bhavesh.

'What about you?' Mehul looked at JD.

'I also haven't had dinner so let's go,' JD stood up.

Mehul and JD moved abreast at a brisk pace. Bhavesh followed them, lagging behind a little because of the metal rod that had been implanted in his left leg after the mishap near the girls' hostel—the one in which he lost his bike but gained the title of FOSLA KING!

On Friday morning, the college bus was supposed to leave for Nahakganj PHC at 8 a.m. sharp. The students started arriving around 9, Dr Sudarshan Shukla, assistant professor of community medicine, in charge of the tour, reached at 9.30 and Bilal Khan, the college bus driver, appeared on the scene at 10.

'Bilal Khan, look how late you are!' Sudarshan Shukla cried out in his high-pitched feminine voice on seeing Bilal climb up to the driver's seat. Bilal didn't bother to acknowledge him. He started the engine and put it in idling mode.

Sudarshan Shukla, nicknamed Chhuara Sir, was very fair with pointy features and spiked hair like that of a porcupine. It was extremely difficult to guess his age, he could be thirty, or he may well be fifty. His health—if you can call it that—qualified him to be classified as a case of PEM (Protein Energy Malnutrition) Grade IV. He was five feet two inches and weighed a pathetic thirty-nine kilograms. He got the monicker of Chhuara, or dried date palm fruit, during a lethal ragging session when he had been a first-year medical student. His seniors named him so because of his skeletal, lifeless frame and the name, Chhuara, stuck over the years in the medical college. With the passage of time and especially after he became an assistant professor, he began to be respectfully addressed as 'Chhuara Sir'. He had gradually accepted the name and, in fact, was now quite comfortable with it, much to the amusement of his students.

Amidst a loud roar of the NMC chant 'Bholay ke bhai bum…' the bus left the shores of the college on its fifty-kilometre journey to PHC, Nahakganj. Maheen Bhai the canteen proprietor, his tall frame swaying from side to side, chased after the bus with a small leather suitcase in his hand. Bilal slowed the bus down and Maheen Bhai jumped in panting badly. He saw that Chhuara Sir was sitting alone on the front seat so he flopped down beside him. As soon as they reached the main road, Bilal Khan pressed the accelerator and the bus zoomed ahead.

'You are very late, Maheen Bhai, I told you the bus will leave at 9 a.m.,' complained Chhuara Sir.

'Look, sir, since I am going home I thought I should buy some balushahi from Narmada Sweets. That's why I got late.' Maheen Bhai was from Nahakganj and his entire family still lived there. Whenever the students went for a field visit to PHC, Nahakganj, Maheen Bhai was always on the bus. He helped to organize the stay and food at Nahakganj and was also able to visit his family.

'*Driver sahib, music-vusic chalao*,' Junaid came up to the driver's seat and requested Bilal Khan.

'Okay, Junaid miyan,' said Bilal Khan, looking back. He knew Junaid's family well.

'Driver sahib, watch out!' shouted Chhuara Sir in a shrill, trembling voice.

Two buffaloes, standing plumb in the middle of the road looked as if they were discussing its pathetic condition. Bilal Khan braked and swerved sharply to the left, avoiding them narrowly. To be a successful driver in this country you require three things: a good horn, good brakes and good luck, not necessarily in that order. Probably good luck should come first.

Chhuara Sir started to hyperventilate but Maheen Bhai was totally unruffled. He had immense faith in Bilal Khan's quicksilver reflexes and cool temperament.

Junaid had held on to the seat in front and was lucky to escape without any injury. 'Play some nice, fast songs,' he requested Bilal again.

'I only have cassettes of old songs, why don't you give me some new cassettes?'

'We don't have any cassettes, we only have CDs.'

'This dabba only plays cassettes,' lamented Bilal Khan.

Junaid went back and settled down in his seat. Bilal Khan pushed a cassette into the player. The player vomited it out. Bilal cursed and shoved it in harder and thumped the front of the player with his fist.

'*Dil ke tukde, tukde karke muskura ke chal diye...*' rang out.

There was a loud protest from the students. They wanted a better song. Bilal ejected the cassette and pushed in another.

'*Ek ladki bheegi bhaagi si...*' Kishore Kumar's vibrant voice couldn't and didn't invite any protests. Most boys sitting at the rear of the bus started to sing along with Kishore Kumar. After an initial hesitation, girls sitting in the front joined in and bettered them with more soulful singing. The seating in the bus was not on gender lines but as the girls were more sincere and had arrived early, they had got the front seats while the boys reaching just in the nick of time were herded at the back. Still JD and the gang had managed seats just a row behind Mansi, Minal and Mita, and were able to pass comments and wisecracks to keep the girls entertained.

By the time side A of the cassette containing assorted Kishore Kumar numbers was over, the bus had reached Sautanpur. Bilal Khan slowed down the bus and parked it in front of Pardesi Dhaba, famous for its gulab jamuns.

'We will stop here for fifteen minutes,' announced Chhuara Sir. 'You can have tea and snacks but remember the bus will leave in exactly fifteen minutes.'

The gulab jamuns floating in thick sugary syrup appeared very inviting. At ₹6 a piece they were a steal. Junaid was the first to buy them. He bought six, two for himself and one each for JD, Lazarus, Manish and Mehul. Mansi and Minal also bought one each and took one careful, calorie-conscious bite, giving away the rest to the puppies loitering below the dhaba charpoy. In the next ten minutes, the entire lot of gulab jamuns at the dhaba was finished.

Maheen Bhai saw JD and the gang climb back into the bus. 'Did you try the gulab jamuns?' he called out.

'Yes, Maheen Bhai. They are really very delicious,' replied JD.

'Sautanpur is famous for gulab jamuns, and Puran Halwai who makes them is even more popular. In this area if anyone wants to eat gulab jamuns he comes to Pardesi Dhaba,' Maheen Bhai informed them.

Bilal Khan jumped into his seat and honked the horn loudly. Within a few minutes everyone was back on their seats and the bus sped off towards its destination. By the time side B of the Kishore Kumar cassette played out, the bus entered Nahakganj.

Nahakganj, with a population of thirty to forty thousand was a typical tehsil town, weather-beaten, sun-baked, congested and filthy. This was the true Bharat, far removed from the India of multiplexes and malls. Haphazardly constructed shops selling cheap clothes, aluminum and brass utensils, auto parts, large fat (not flat) television sets, cycles, grocery items and sweets lined both sides of the roads. Nahakganj Hospital was situated just behind the row of shops on the left side and behind the hospital was the bus stand. In the non-stop racket there was no chance of patients ever getting bored.

Bilal Khan parked the bus in the hospital compound near an old battered ambulance that must have seen better days. Now its rusted body rested on four sets of bricks instead of wheels. Obviously, the money supposed to be spent on its maintenance was siphoned off by some people putting up false bills.

Chhuara Sir got down from the bus and went inside the hospital. If people from the archaeology department had seen the hospital building, they would have immediately recommended it to be included in the list of world heritage monuments. Whether the single-storeyed hospital building was a relic of the Mughal period or a gift of the British empire was difficult to say. Repeated repairs and unplanned additions of small rooms had totally changed its initial architecture, if it had any to begin with.

A dark, fat, clean-shaven guy with an impressive belly tumbled out of the hospital and approached the bus. Beside him Chhuara Sir looked like a sidecar attached to a bullet motorcycle. Most of the students had got down from the bus and were standing in small groups under the shade of a verdant neem tree.

'I am Dr Hasmukh Kumar, Block Medical Officer and in-charge of the Nahakganj PHC. I will give you a brief round of the hospital and then you can have lunch in the common hall of the trainees' hostel where you all will put up for the next two days.'

'Come on, boys and girls, see a functioning PHC with your own eyes.' After Dr Hasmukh's gruff voice, Chhuara Sir's shrill tone appeared as if Lata Mangeshkar was singing a duet with Hemant Kumar.

'What's the need to shout? We are not about to witness the launch of a space shuttle,' Junaid whispered in JD's ear.

'Don't bet on it, this experience could be even more shocking,' sighed JD.

Wild shrubs, tall grass and a green algae-covered pond full of bathing buffaloes made it seem like an African safari rather than an educational trip to a PHC. If Nahakganj Hospital somehow missed out in the race for the world heritage site label, it would certainly be declared as the most eco-friendly hospital.

As is their wont, several girls including Minal, Mansi and Meeta rushed up and started to follow Dr Hasmukh closely. He was not leading them to witness neurosurgery but it didn't matter, a habit is a habit is a... The boys as usual remained in the background, seemingly more interested in the roundness of the buttocks and swaying of the hips of the girls than in the demands of their noble profession.

Tobacco- and paan-chewers of Nahakganj had taken great

pains to cover the bare walls of the corridors with modern art. Even M. F. Husain would have found it difficult to paint such complex figures in such vibrant colours.

'Why does no one believe in saving electricity?' Dr Hasmukh grumbled on seeing a naked bulb hanging from the ceiling, burning brightly. He went up to the switchboard and tried to switch off the bulb. The switch was an antique piece and probably with increasing age had developed arthritis. It refused to budge! Dr Hasmukh gave up after a few futile efforts. Obviously, nothing less than a sledgehammer would have helped to switch off the bulb.

Dr Hasmukh came to an abrupt stop at the T-junction and waited for the students to catch up. 'This is my room,' he pointed with apparent pride towards the room situated right at the junction. 'Sitting here, I can keep an eye on everything that goes on in the hospital.' A small, black, wooden nameplate with Dr Hasmukh's name, degree and designation painted on it in white was affixed on the top of the door.

'Next to it is Dr Laltaram's room, then Dr Rajeev Ranjan Sharma's and the last one is Dr Shailja's. At the end of the corridor is the labour room,' Dr Hasmukh informed them, turning to the left.

Both Dr Laltaram and Dr Rajeev Ranjan Sharma were absent from their respective rooms. A few patients were loitering around in the corridor. They were not really sick, but habitual visitors. The really sick ones had already gone to the two doctors' staff quarters located within the campus. Both Dr Laltaram and Dr R. R. Sharma believed in serving ailing humanity. For them the place was immaterial. What difference does it make if you serve the people at home or in hospital?

Mansi and Minal went ahead and peeped inside the labour room. It was so dark in there that the only way you could be sure the baby had come out was by its crying. Most labour rooms in the government hospitals can easily obtain an ISI (Indian Standard Institute, not Inter Service Intelligence of Pakistan) certification for maintaining a uniform standard of filthiness at all times.

Dr Hasmukh started to walk back in the opposite direction. 'This is the injection-cum-dressing room and opposite to it is the OT (operation theatre),' he pointed first to his left, then to his right.

A rickety metal table covered with a tattered green mackintosh stood in the middle of the injection room. By its side was a small, square wooden table on top of which was a big open jar containing yellow Furacin ointment. It seemed Furacin ointment was the preferred breakfast choice for the hospital flies. The flies were diving in and out of the jar with not a care in the world. Their apparent health was direct proof that the ointment was entirely harmless.

Dr Hasmukh pushed at the OT door with his right shoulder, using his considerable weight. 'Chheeeiii...eeeiii...' the door opened slowly with a blood-curdling noise. The strong gust of wind entering through the shattered windowpanes hit the students in the face. A family of homing pigeons flew away through the open ventilators with a loud flapping of wings. Two bats hanging from the roof didn't pay any attention and kept sleeping peacefully. Large spiders busy building complicated webs also continued with their work without giving a damn.

The dust-covered OT light hanging by a metal chain from the ceiling looked as if it had been sentenced to death a hundred years ago. The OT table had collapsed and was lying in a heap on the floor. It was rumoured that most of the patients fainted on entering the OT and anaesthesia was never required. All in all the setting was perfect for the shooting of a horror film. Someone please inform Ramsay Brothers and Ram Gopal Varma.

'Don't get alarmed, the OT is closed for renovation,' Dr

Hasmukh tried to assure the students. The truth was the OT had been under renovation for the past five years. You see, everything in this country works according to a five-year plan.

Dr Hasmukh led the students to the other wing of the hospital in which the meeting hall and the male and female wards were located. 'The weekly and monthly meetings of health workers regarding various national health programmes are held here,' he pointed towards the locked doors of the meeting hall. He moved up further ahead, 'This is the...'

'Female ward,' JD said, looking at the saris, petticoats, blouses and other assorted feminine clothes hanging on a clothes line outside the ward.

'And this is the...' Dr Hasmukh pointed in the opposite direction.

'Male ward,' Junaid said, eyeing the shirts, pyjamas, underwear and vests drying near the entrance of the ward. Both JD and Junaid were close behind Dr Hasmukh.

At the end of the corridor, Dr Hasmukh exited through a metal grill door into the back courtyard and stopped in front of a dilapidated structure with crumbling walls. The central part of the roof had caved in during torrential rains a few years back and had never been repaired. He stood there, waiting for the students to gather around him.

'This is the PM or the postmortem room,' Dr Hasmukh patted the cracked wall of the decrepit room with affection. Who wouldn't? After all, postmortems were sources of substantial income. Dr Hasmukh was a God-fearing man and he believed in fair play. He took money from both parties, the murderer and the murdered, and then wrote an honest, unbiased report sticking to what he actually found during the PM.

'If you want to work in a PHC, you must know how to perform PMs,' said Dr Hasmukh, pulling up his trousers, which had a propensity to fall down from his paunch every few minutes. 'You may not know how to treat a living person, but you must know how to perform a PM on a dead body.'

'Why is knowing how to perform a PM so important in rural hospitals?' Junaid asked, a bit intrigued.

Dr Hasmukh smiled benevolently. A few drops of the gutkha he was chewing trickled down from the corners of his mouth and fell on his shirt, leaving brownish stains. 'People in places like Nahakganj don't have any work between the rabi and kharif crops. How long can people sit idle? Nahakganjis are a peculiar breed, so instead of killing time they start killing each other.' Dr Hasmukh paused for effect. 'When people get killed, they will have to undergo a postmortem. It's as simple as that!'

Dr Hasmukh said 'undergo a postmortem' with so much pride, it appeared as if he was saying 'undergo an angioplasty' or 'undergo a renal transplant'.

Jhingamal Patel, the hospital peon, was lurking in the background. Dr Hasmukh signalled to him to open the PM room. Jhinga was polio-affected and used a stick to move around the hospital. He could be called a mobile advertisement for the Pulse Polio campaign. Jhinga hobbled up to the door and opened the lock after struggling with it for a few minutes.

Several boys and girls rushed in to see the most important room of the hospital. The floor was made of chipped white tiles, the walls were a dirty grey and the roof had a gaping hole at its centre. Everything has its advantages and disadvantages. If the hole created problems during the rains, it was of great value during the rest of the year. Nahakganj, like most other villages, was always without electricity. This helped villagers kill each other during the night and during the day, the natural light entering through the hole helped doctors to perform PMs on them.

The hole in the roof had other advantages as well. If you were lying on the PM table, you could get a direct view of heaven. So it could be called 'A Room With A View'. Also, if due to any reason the soul remained entrapped in the dead body, it was liberated during the dissection of the body and unified with other souls in heaven.

'Okay, boys and girls, it's enough for today,' announced Dr Hasmukh, pulling up his trousers over his paunch. 'You can now go to the trainees' hostel and have lunch. You are free in the evening, so enjoy yourselves.'

'Sir, where is the nearest disco?' asked a male voice from the rear.

'Which pub do you recommend?' asked another, amid a roar of laughter.

Dr Hasmukh was always game for fun and jokes. 'There is a desi liquour shop nearby. They have Kesar, Rose, Kewda and Laung. But my recommendation is Kewda. As far as a disco is concerned, I am sorry, but you can go to Laxmi Talkies and watch the hit Bhojpuri film, *Raani Ka Kaata Na Maange Paani*.' Then he turned and walked off, singing his favourite Bhojpuri song.

During lunch, Chhuara Sir called out for everyone's attention. 'Listen everybody! Dr Hasmukh has informed me that under the male sterilization drive tomorrow, they are holding a VT, that is, a vasectomy camp, at Nahakganj Hospital. Your batch is extremely lucky as you will be able to witness several VT operations.'

'In that OT?' JD asked in horror.

'No! A makeshift OT has been readied in the mating room,' he smiled, pronouncing meeting as mating. He was well aware of the condition of the main OT since he had been coming to Nahakganj Hospital for the last three years.

'They have put up a steel table and an instrument trolley there.'

⊕

It seemed not many men in Nahakganj were willing to get their sperm-carrying duct (vas deferens) chopped off (-ectomy). They feared that it might interfere with the only pastime they had in such a dull place. As a result, only thirteen cases had been registered by 10 a.m. on the day of the camp.

'How many VT cases have matured?' Dr Hasmukh asked Mangtulal Malviya, the male health supervisor, on reaching the hospital. His manner was such as if he were asking about bank FDs.

'Thirteen,' the buck-toothed health supervisor replied.

'You mean *only* thirteen! The collector of this district will be enraged, we are way behind the target,' wailed Dr Hasmukh.

'We tried our best, doctor sahib. I am still hopeful we may get a few more cases,' Mangtulal's voice lacked conviction.

Dr Hasmukh nodded. 'Go ask Chhuara Sir to bring in the students. We will start the VT operations shortly.'

The VT operations started soon after, and the students in groups of five to six went in to watch them. Dr Hasmukh was an old hand at doing these operations and this was evident in the speed and ease with which he did his job. In the next hour and a half he had done ten VTs, when Jhinga hopped in.

'Sir, SDM Rawat sahib has come to meet you. I told him you are doing VT operations but he says it is urgent,' Jhinga smiled wickedly. Everyone in Nahakganj Hospital knew the overbearing SDM (sub-divisional magistrate) had piles.

'Okay, I'll attend to him. You go and tell Dr Laltaram to finish off the remaining cases.' Dr Hasmukh removed his bloodstained gloves but let the cap and mask remain. This was done to send a subtle message to the SDM that he was doing something more important than signing some obscure files. He was quite adept at dealing with people with bloated estimates of self-importance and Rawat had a massive ego problem. Dr Hasmukh was also an expert on piles and had provided relief to several people suffering from it.

No sooner had Dr Hasmukh left than Dr Laltaram rushed in. He had returned recently from VT training in the department of surgery at NMC, Bhopla, and was itching to try out his newly acquired skills. He put on the cap, mask and surgical gloves supplied to him by Nurse Mary Jones. Picking up the scalpel, he slowly surveyed his audience, which comprised JD, Junaid, Lazarus, Manish, Mehul and a few others. JD and the gang had played cards till the wee hours of the morning and had woken up very late. They were among the last few students to witness the VT operations.

'Is this the first time you are watching a VT operation?' Dr Laltaram asked Lazarus, wielding the scalpel as if it was the sword of Tipu Sultan.

'Yes, sir.'

'Okay, then watch carefully as I operate.'

'But, sir, isn't the patient a bit too old to undergo the sterilization operation?' Lazarus asked in a hushed voice. 'He looks well over sixty!'

'Never doubt the reproductive power of an Indian male, you will get a rude shock! This fellow here can still create a lot of mischief,' said Dr Laltaram, injecting Xylocaine, an anaesthetic, in the scrotum of the patient.

'Now watch carefully.' Dr Laltaram made an incision about one inch in size with his scalpel. He then inserted an artery forceps through the opening and started to search for the right-sided vas deferens. After three to four attempts, he got hold of something, which he pulled out with obvious glee. He didn't bother whether it was the tube to be cut or merely blood vessels. He cut it off promptly and somehow managed to stop the bleeding. He then chopped off something on the left side and stitched up the wound. He was sweating heavily. If a five-minute job takes fifty you are bound to sweat. JD and his friends bit back their amusement.

Dr Laltaram struggled a bit with the next patient too and began sweating even more.

'Got it!' Dr Laltaram shouted triumphantly and chopped off the vas deferens before it could slip out of his grasp again. But God only knew what he had cut because a jet of blood hit him on his bulbous nose, throwing him out of kilter. In a bout of panic, Dr Laltaram stitched up the wound. Nurse Mary Jones applied the dressing and sent the patient out.

Just then Dr Hasmukh entered the makeshift OT. 'If you are finished, let's go for lunch.'

'There is still one case left,' said Dr Laltaram in a harassed voice.

'What? You did two VTs in one hour?'

'Sir, I still haven't quite got the hang of it. Will you finish off the last VT?' Dr Laltaram pleaded.

'Okay,' said Dr Hasmukh, briskly putting on the gloves and mask.

This time JD and the gang got to see how VT should actually be done. Dr Laltaram stood subserviently, quietly observing the master surgeon at work. The case was over in exactly eight minutes from incision to stitches.

⊕

Around 7 p.m., Mehul informed JD that Chhuara Sir was looking for him.

'What does he want?' JD yawned.

Mehul merely shrugged his shoulders.

'Where is he at the moment?' JD didn't show much interest in meeting Chhuara Sir.

'He is having tea at a small kiosk just outside the hospital gate,' Mehul replied.

'I also want to have tea. I think I'll go and meet him there.' JD got up and stretched his arms above his head. 'Anyone interested in having tea?' Junaid and Lazarus raised their hands and they all got up and went in search of Chhuara Sir and tea.

'You wanted to talk to me?' JD asked Chhuara Sir who was smoking a Wills Navy Cut after finishing his tea.

'Ah, yes,' said Chhuara Sir, exhaling a steady stream of cigarette smoke. He looked extremely cute in that pose. One cigarette enjoying the other... 'Dr Hasmukh is hosting a small party at his residence. He has asked me to bring along a few students also. Are you interested?'

'Sure, why not? As it is, we don't have much to do in this wilderness.' JD perked up.

'Yes, let's enjoy tonight, tomorrow we leave for Bhopla.' Chhuara Sir appeared to be in a bright mood. 'You two also come along.' He blew some more smoke in Lazarus and Junaid's faces.

When JD, Lazarus and Junaid arrived at Dr Hasmukh's place with Chhuara Sir, Maheen Bhai was already there doing what he did best, looking after the arrangements. Jhinga was hopping around energetically trying to help Maheen Bhai. Shortly after, Dr Laltaram and Dr R. R. Sharma arrived and the introductions began. Practically everyone was from NMC, Bhopla, except Dr R. R. Sharma who was from Jabarpur.

The party had been arranged in the small front lawn of Dr Hasmukh's official residence inside the hospital campus. After a brief chitchat, Dr Hasmukh got up from his chair and opened a bottle of Old Monk Rum. 'Today I have decided to serve rum cola just to relive the good old hostel days. If anyone wants to have whisky, we also have a full bottle of Peter Scotch right here.'

He pointed towards the centre table on which the bottles and glasses were kept.

Dr Hasmukh must have drunk not less than fifty bottles of Peter Scot in his drinking career spanning well over thirty years but he still insisted upon calling it Peter Scotch. Either he had never bothered to read the label on the bottle or he sincerely believed it to be true Scotch from Scotland. Either way it didn't matter as everyone settled for rum cola. Junaid didn't drink, so he settled for cola minus rum.

'Is there some special occasion today?' asked Dr Laltaram, gulping down the tasty brew.

'*Jashn-e-Aazaadi!* Celebration of independence!' Dr Hasmukh raised his glass and started to laugh in his trademark jerky style. It was less of a laugh and more of a series of loud hiccups.

'So, Bhabhiji has gone to Jhansi!' Dr Laltaram remarked.

'Where else would Jhansi ki Rani go? To her hometown, of course,' Dr Hasmukh kept on hiccupping. Chhuara Sir joined in with his shrill laughter as if Dr Hasmukh had cracked the funniest joke. Chhuara Sir had a reputation of getting drunk with the third sip he took (and not the third peg). Looking at his BMI (Body Mass Index) it was not altogether impossible.

Maheen Bhai brought a tray laden with chicken tangdi kebabs and served everybody. Dr Hasmukh filled the empty glasses with rum cola again.

'Your tangdi kebabs are too good!' Dr Laltaram sucked clean a chicken leg and tossed it over his shoulder in the lantana shrub.

'My tangdi kebabs won't taste so good. They are chickens', that is why they are so delicious,' Maheen Bhai cracked a silly joke. Everyone ignored it but Chhuara Sir went into another fit of uncontrolled shrieks.

After a third round of rum cola, Maheen Bhai announced that dinner was ready. Chhuara Sir was fast approaching the final stage of a coma and even JD and Lazarus were feeling the ill effects of the strong cocktail that Dr Hasmukh had prepared. Dr R. R. Sharma had already called it quits after the second round. Only Dr Laltaram and Dr Hasmukh were still drinking steadily.

'Maheen Bhai, food later. First let's hear a Ghalib's shair in English from Dr Hasmukh. Sir, please recite Ghalib's shair in English,' requested Dr Laltaram. It was besides the point that he neither understood Urdu nor could he speak much English.

'Okay, okay!' Dr Hasmukh gulped down the remaining rum cola in his glass.

> Ishk ne Ghalib nikamma kar diya,
> Varna hum bhi aadmi thhe, kaam ke.

'Now the English translation,' Dr Hasmukh looked at the troika of JD, Junaid and Lazarus.

> This bloody love has made me useless,
> Otherwise I was the man of PWD.

Everybody burst out laughing, Dr Laltaram the loudest, probably because he had drunk the most. When it came to consuming free liquor, Dr Laltaram was peerless.

The menu was not elaborate but the food was sumptuous, especially the mutton rogan josh prepared by Maheen Bhai. Phirni, again a specialty of Maheen Bhai, was the perfect end to a great evening.

Suddenly, Chhuara Sir jerked out of his chair and started to shout. 'Ghosts! Ghosts! Run!'

'Have you gone mad? There are no ghosts here. Everyone dreads Nahakganj Hospital. Even the ghosts!' Dr Hasmukh pushed Chhuara Sir back into his chair.

'Something is moving there,' Junaid pointed towards the hospital campus gate.

'I can see two white shapes progressing slowly in this direction,' whispered Lazarus.

Certainly, as everyone looked, two white figures with their legs wide apart were moving in their direction slowly. They leaned to the left, then right, then left, then to… Their progress was painfully slow. The white sheets draped over their shoulders were fluttering in the late night breeze. The rum cola levels went down as the fear factor rose up. The group remained huddled together, looking apprehensively at the two white undulating figures.

'Oye bhencho!' The hiccupping started as Dr Hasmukh solved the riddle. This was not the first time nor would it be the last, when after a vasectomy, patients had developed huge, coconut-sized scrotal haematoceles (blood-filled swelling). The figures in white were the two cases done by Dr Laltaram. Along with the sperm ducts, he had also chopped off several small and large blood vessels, some of which he had tied successfully and others he had failed to do so. This resulted in continuous oozing of blood and plasma in the scrotal sac, resulting in the development of a large, tense and painful swelling of the scrotum. Because the scrotum had enlarged considerably, the patients were walking slowly with their legs wide apart. They were indeed ghosts that would keep revisiting Dr Laltaram's conscience for a long, long time.

'Take them to the hospital. I'll come in a minute and see what can be done to help them,' Dr Hasmukh tersely instructed Jhinga.

The party was over in a jiffy as everyone dispersed quickly. Chhuara Sir was literally carried on their shoulders by JD and Lazarus to his sleeping quarters. Dr Hasmukh went in, splashed some water on his face to revive his dulled senses and rushed to the hospital to attend to his patients who were in much pain and discomfort. Putting on a pair of surgical gloves, he removed as much blood as he could with the help of a wide-bore 18-number needle attached to a 20-ml syringe. He then smeared the scrotal swelling liberally with magsulf and applied a tight bandage over it.

'Start an intravenous drip and give them an injection of Voveran. Tomorrow we will refer them to the department of surgery, NMC, Bhopla,' Dr Hasmukh instructed the night-duty nurse before leaving for his residence.

Next morning, the college bus finally departed from Nahakganj for Bhopla at 10.30 a.m. JD and Mansi were sitting on neighbouring seats across the aisle. Their eyes met several times and their gaze lingered on each other indeterminately. JD couldn't fathom the message hidden in Mansi's eyes but when she smiled, it lifted the shadows surrounding his heart.

The ongoing round of the singing game, antakshari, was not yet over when Bilal Khan drove the bus through the gates of the college campus.

20
FOSLA Hall of Fame

It had been a week since the students' trip to Nahakganj. JD, Junaid and Lazarus had bunked the ophthalmology class and were sitting in the college canteen sipping tea. Maheen Bhai slid in beside JD on a vacant seat. He had a worried expression on his face. 'How is Tarun Gupta? Has he regained consciousness?'

'Why? What happened to him?' JD asked looking surprised.

'Don't you know he consumed Valium tablets last night and was admitted to the ICU in an unconscious state?' Maheen Bhai prided himself in keeping abreast of the college gossip, most of which anyway took place under the roof of the college canteen.

'Well, what could be the reason? The results of the senior finals came out almost a week ago and, expectedly, Tarun had topped,' mused JD.

'Yes, you can't help it. You have to top if you are the dean's son,' added Junaid.

'Immediately after the results were out, his girlfriend Simran Saxena ditched him. She is now engaged to an industrialist's son,' Maheen Bhai informed them.

'But why did she do that? They were going steady for close to four years now and, thanks to Dean Dr S. L. Gupta's influence, she constantly obtained very good marks in almost all subjects.' Lazarus was still trying to come to terms with the news.

'Yes, she was third in the merit list in the senior final exam,' said Junaid. 'That's the least Dr S. L. Gupta could do for his future daughter-in-law.'

'That's exactly the reason! Simran no more needed the dean's influence so she showed Tarun Gupta the door. He was merely a pawn she used to further her career, and the idiot fell for the ploy.' Maheen Bhai summarized the whole matter.

'You mean, all along Simran was making a fool of Tarun?' asked Lazarus.

'That's quite obvious, otherwise why would she ditch him just after the final exams?' said Maheen Bhai pragmatically.

'That's what happens to over-smart people,' commented Junaid.

'It's quite true, most of the time Tarun behaved as if he and not his father was the dean,' said Lazarus.

'Whatever. I am still not convinced. Tarun is too haraami a fellow to die for a girl,' proclaimed JD.

'You mean Tarun is doing all this to pressurize Simran into reconsidering her decision?' asked Lazarus.

'I don't know for sure. Maybe he did consume ten to twenty Valium tablets on the spur of the moment. But whatever little I know of Simran, she seems too tough a nut to crack under these silly pressure tactics adopted by Tarun,' replied JD.

'Maybe Tarun did love Simran and couldn't bear the shock. You know girls can really drive you crazy,' opined Junaid as if he was an expert on such matters.

'Let's go to the ICU and find out for ourselves—maybe Tarun has already regained consciousness,' suggested Lazarus.

The three of them stood up and left for the ICU.

'Keep me informed!' shouted Maheen Bhai.

'Will do!' JD shouted back.

JD, Junaid and Lazarus had no difficulty gaining entrance to the ICU located on the third floor of the main hospital block.

White aprons and dangling stethos were their passports to the sanctum sanctorum. They removed their shoes in the anteroom and searched for the ICU slippers. Failing to find any, they walked in barefoot. It probably was an apt introduction to the government's plans of turning them into barefoot doctors.

Two rows of ten cubicles each, with a nursing station in between and an in-duty doctor's chamber at the end, was the basic layout of the ICU. The doctor's table was littered with patient files, X-rays and blood reports. The air conditioners were making a lot of noise without really being able to do much cooling. Still, the ICU environment was much better than the hot, sultry conditions existing outside. The rhythmic hiss of the ventilators and the intermittent beeps of the monitors were certainly mesmerizing. The trio kept standing in the passage, uncertain of whom to approach as there was nobody in sight.

'What do you want?' asked a senior ICU nurse emerging out of cubicle number four. She had immediately recognized them as student intruders. Senior nurses are quite intolerant of the undergraduate students and the nurses posted in the ICU are almost paranoid about the latter's presence among critically ill patients. They are somehow suffered because there is no other way the medical students would learn how to handle seriously ill patients.

'Hello, JD!' said Dr Deepak Bhargav, resident medical officer, coming out of the same cubicle. 'I presume you have come to see Tarun Gupta. He is in cubicle number seven.'

'How is he?' JD asked.

'Stable. Still heavily sedated but all his vitals are normal. I think he should start gaining consciousness tonight.'

'How many tablets did he consume?'

'Probably twenty, because two empty strips of Valium 5 were lying on the floor under his bed.'

'How bad is that?'

'Twenty tablets will certainly not kill him. Moreover, he was brought here well in time. Initially he had some respiratory depression and low blood pressure but with CPAP (Continuous Positive Airway Pressure) and a dopamine drip, his vitals stabilized fairly quickly. Now his oxygen saturation and blood pressure are normal even after discontinuing CPAP and the dopamine drip.'

'So you are waiting for the kidneys to wash out the drug?'

'Exactly. Meanwhile we are giving him a slow dextrose saline drip to provide him nutrition and to maintain hydration.'

'Can we see him?'

'Why not! Call out his name, who knows, he might respond to you guys,' said Dr Deepak Bhargav before leaving them and entering cubicle number five.

JD, Junaid and Lazarus entered cubicle number seven. Tarun Gupta appeared to be fast asleep, his chest going up and down, slowly and evenly. A monitor attached to his left arm showed his blood pressure, pulse and oxygen saturation. An intravenous line attached to his right arm delivered dextrose saline to his bloodstream. In his sleep, Tarun's coarse features, thick lips and bulbous nose didn't look that jarring. Sleep probably smoothens a lot of rough edges turning a not-so-pleasant face into a more likeable one. If he would not have been lying on a hospital bed, Tarun could easily be mistaken for taking a quick nap.

JD went up to Tarun's side and bending down, called his name. 'Tarun, sir! Wake up, open your eyes.'

There was a slight flickering of Tarun's eyelids but his eyes remained closed.

'Just tell him Simran is standing outside the ICU crying,' whispered Junaid in JD's ear.

'Shut up and behave. This is no time to crack jokes,' reprimanded JD.

'I am not joking. Just tell him Simran is waiting for him at the Fun Cinemas and he will be there in five minutes flat,' persisted Junaid.

'Let's all go out, there is no point standing here debating whether he is bluffing or not,' said JD, leaving the cubicle.

'Even if he is a fake, it requires guts to put one's reputation at stake for a girl,' interjected Lazarus sombrely.

'Yes, even I am surprised. Watching his father bend before every politician and bureaucrat, I thought Tarun too had only two orifices, one to feed and the other to fart with no guts in between,' smirked Junaid, putting on his shoes in the anteroom.

'Come, let's go to the hostel. Or do you want to attend Dr Gulani's ENT class in the afternoon?' JD asked.

'Not today, but some other day, surely. Everyone says you must attend Dr Gulani's class otherwise your medical college experience is incomplete,' said Junaid, his eyes lighting up with perverse pleasure.

'Why? What's so great about it?' inquired Lazarus.

'It's the only class where the students put a lock from the outside so that the teacher doesn't run away midway through the lecture,' replied Junaid.

Lazarus smacked his lips in anticipation. 'That's something!'

Whatever the reason for Tarun's action, increasing suicide attempts in college campuses across the country is a worrisome phenomenon. Poor academic performance, failure to get placements and lovers' tiffs, all contribute to this disturbing trend. More rational expectations from parents and reducing societal pressure will go a long way in controlling this menace.

⊕

Prem Arora, the undeclared president of FOSLA, had called a meeting of frustoos to discuss the ramifications of Tarun Gupta's action. He didn't want any setbacks to the organization he had given his sweat (chasing after girls), semen (wet dreams) and blood (getting beaten on two occasions by the relatives of the girls). The members started arriving in the UG mess around 5 p.m. and soon all the chairs were taken up. They were from different batches, right from the juniormost to the most senior. Frustoos are a unified lot, they have one religion, one aim and one ambition: to somehow patao an XX-chromosome-harbouring specimen.

Prem Arora stood up and looked at the substantial gathering with satisfaction. He was especially pleased with the presence of Bhavesh Mehta (FOSLA King) and Rajveer Tomar ('Langad'). 'Friends, as you all know, we are gathered here in a moment of great crisis. Dear Tarun Gupta is admitted in the ICU in a grave condition and you all know the reason why.'

'Yes, because the cart changed the horse,' someone commented.

'How long can you remain hitched to a pony?' remarked another.

'Silence, please! Although I agree he should not have taken such a drastic step, still we should not poke fun at one of our own.'

'Prem Bhai, you didn't provide him good coaching. Look at you—even after twelve solid rejections you are still going great guns. And look at Tarun, he is in the ICU after the first setback,' Mannu Sharma blamed Prem.

'No personal comments,' reminded Prem. 'Let's hear some positive suggestions about how best to cope with the trauma of this inevitable, recurring tragedy.'

'Let's develop a support group on the lines of Alcoholics Anonymous and name it Frustoholics Fuckonymous,' suggested FOSLA King Bhavesh Mehta.

'Why don't we have regular booze parties to help our heartbroken members overcome the catastrophe of rejection,' opined Rajveer Tomar, 'Langad'.

'That way we will end up having two or three binges every week with no money left for other activities,' argued Danav Sisodia.

'Why don't we all say "fuck off" to the girls and develop more self-reliance,' Ghanshyam Prasad smiled sheepishly.

'Bhencho, you fuck off,' shouted Rajeev Gaur agitatedly. There was a strong rumour that Rajeev Gaur was on the verge of succeeding in his constant endeavour to hook Anjali Trivedi, a dusky beauty from his immediate junior batch. His anguish and loss of temper was amply understood and reasonably well accepted by the frustoos.

'No fighting, please! Let Ghanshyam Prasad elaborate upon the point he just made,' Prem Arora intervened.

'Yes, let's hear what you mean by self-reliance,' winked Mannu Sharma.

'Well, blue films and you know what…' Ghanshyam Prasad nodded with a knowing glance at the gathering and stormed off in disgust. There was a momentary silence followed by an uproar, which threatened to end the meeting.

'Calm down! No laughing,' Prem Arora said, laughing uncontrollably.

'Ass! He thinks only he is smart but we are smarter and better practitioners of that art,' declared Danav Sisodia.

'Be serious, one of our own is still not out of the ICU. At least show some respect for his daring act,' chided Prem Arora.

'Yes, his name would have been included in the Hall of Fame in olden times,' remarked Rajeev Gaur in all seriousness.

'What do you mean?' Bhavesh Mehta asked.

'I mean, like you have Heer-Ranjha, Sohni-Mahiwal, Laila-Majnu, there well might have been a Tarun-Simran saga as well,' Rajeev was still serious. Prem Arora was nodding furiously in total agreement.

'The Kareena-Shahid Kapoor love story is more like it,' Mannu gave his informed opinion. 'And why not call it the Hall of Infamy?'

'We are again digressing from the purpose for which we have collected here,' Prem Arora had a pained expression on his face.

'So why don't you spell out a strategy? That is, if you have any,' said Mannu.

'If I had a foolproof plan, I would have been married a dozen times by now and not be lying in bed alone night after night, relying on self-reliance,' said Prem Arora, a bit irritated.

'I tell you, there is only one way of dealing with such haughty girls. We do it all the time in Bhind-Morena,' Rajveer Tomar stood up and raised both his hands to quieten down the boisterous gathering.

'And what is that?' Prem Arora asked.

'Kidnap them!' smiled Rajveer Tomar.

'And who is going to do the kidnapping, you, saale 'Langad'. You won't even reach the outskirts of Bhopla before the police will get you,' rebuked Mannu Sharma.

'He has forgotten that his dacoit ancestors, Grandpa Mohar Singh and Grandma Putli Bai, are long dead,' commented Rajeev Gaur.

'You madar...' hollered Tomar.

'You bhen...' retaliated Gaur.

All hell broke loose. In the bedlam, Prem Arora fell down on the floor and was trampled upon, dragged through the door and thrown out of the mess. Blows were exchanged between Tomar, Gaur and Mannu and the meeting terminated abruptly.

But Tarun Gupta's name entered the FOSLA Hall of Fame, permanently and indelibly.

21
Dr Gulani's ENT Class

'Don't miss today's ENT class, it's going to be a riot.' The SMS was circulating since early morning. JD forwarded it to Mansi.

'I have no intention of missing it,' replied Mansi.

'I missed you,' JD messaged again. Mansi had gone home to Pune for a week to attend the marriage of her cousin and had returned the previous evening.

There was no reply. This had been the problem right through. Mansi had never been very forthcoming about their relationship. There always remained an element of uncertainty, which disturbed JD. Several times he had thought of confronting Mansi with the question uppermost in his mind—'Do you love me?' On each occasion he had developed cold feet. Probably he, too, wanted to let the question remain unanswered. What if she said a definitive 'No'?

JD had no doubts about his feelings for Mansi. But did she feel the same way? He was not so sure. He knew she liked him but there is a vast stretch of unfathomable deep sea between liking and loving. You may be on two shores hundreds of miles apart and still be deeply in love. Or you may be stranded on the same island and still feel light years apart. There are no set rules, no defined parameters and no profound explanations for the feeling called love. People simply fall in love or they don't.

Immersed in the vortex of his troubled feelings for Mansi, JD entered the classroom. He was in for a big surprise. The entire lecture theatre was crammed with students as if Salman Khan and not Dr Gulani were taking the class. Several seniors were present in the crowd and had obviously come to have some fun. JD could recognize Mannu Sharma, Rajeev Gaur, Shantanu Sikarwar and Danav Sisodia sitting at the back.

Rajveer Tomar and Ghanshyam Prasad were lurking in the corridor waiting for Dr Gulani to enter the classroom so that they could lock it from outside. All the lecture theatres had a narrow door at the rear for an emergency exit. They planned to get in through it after locking Dr Gulani inside with the marauding mass of students.

After an interminable delay, Dr Gulani walked in wearing his trademark sweater with loud grey and brown checks. It had large, round, dark brown buttons in the centre and two square pockets lower down on either side. Dr Gulani wore this sweater to the hospital every day beginning from 1 October to 28 February. The duration was increased by one day, ending on 29 February, during a leap year. He had been doing it for the past twenty years without fail. It was not as if he couldn't afford another sweater, he was such a nondescript person he felt lost without his checked sweater. In fact, the college staff and even his family would have turned him out if he had tried to enter his home without his sweater.

Everything about Dr Gulani was unremarkable—his complexion, his features, his voice, his walk, his posture—except his unique sweater, and most likely that made him cling to it all the time. Although it didn't have a barcode, one swipe at its collar with the barcode reader and the monitor screen would have flashed Dr Gulani in bold lettering.

Dr Gulani was well ahead of his times as far as wearing trousers was concerned. Low-waisted jeans have been in vogue for only the past few years but Dr Gulani had been wearing ultra low-waisted trousers since time immemorial. What stopped them from falling off his waist was a mystery even Agatha Christie and Perry Mason would have loved to solve.

Dr Gulani went straight to the podium and tried to conceal himself behind it. He did it quite successfully too, because only his bespectacled face was now visible. This was a necessary precaution to protect himself from the enemy fire which could start from any part of the large lecture theatre. He never took attendance because no one ever missed his class. Everyone attended to participate in the fun and games. He never brought any notes to teach because he knew no one came to be taught.

'Today's topic is sinusitis,' started Dr Gulani in a faltering voice. 'It is the inflammation of the sinuses surrounding the nose, also known as paranasal sinuses. These are maxillary, frontal and ethamoidal.'

'Sir, please write the names of the sinuses on the blackboard, we want to take notes,' Danav Sisodia spoke from the third row.

'No, I will not write anything on the board, you try to take notes as I speak.'

'But sir, why?' Danav asked innocently, hiding a piece of chalk in his right hand.

'You know the answer very well,' Dr Gulani ducked behind the podium even more so that only his bespectacled eyes were visible.

'I don't understand sir, I am attending your class for the first time,' Danav was the epitome of sincerity.

'Don't try to fool me, I have seen you here before.'

'Sir, we really want to take notes. Please write down the names of various sinuses on the board,' Minal Patnaik spoke sweetly from the second row. Even good girls had a mischievous streak to them, mused Mehul. He looked back and winked at her from the first row.

Dr Gulani fell for the deep dimples on Minal's pretty face as she smiled at him. He left his bunker and walked towards the board, treading gingerly. He had not even finished writing the 'S' of the word sinusitis when three chalk pieces hit him on the back of his head and several more struck his back. Two low flying MiG 29s crashed against the blackboard. Dr Gulani dived behind the podium for safety.

Gradually, his head emerged from behind the stand. 'From now onwards I am not going to write anything on the blackboard,' he declared with an authority he did not feel he possessed.

Suddenly Shantanu Sikarwar caught hold of Rajveer Tomar and came rushing towards Dr Gulani, 'Sir, he is disturbing me. He is not letting me take notes. He has stolen my pen.'

'No sir, he is disturbing me,' cried Rajveer Tomar in a funny manner.

Then both of them started hitting each other. That the blows were patently fake and innocuous was obvious to all, except Dr Gulani. He jumped out of his bomb shelter and tried to separate the fighting duo. All of a sudden, Tomar and Sikarwar let go of each other and caught hold of Dr Gulani's legs, Tomar on the left side and Sikarwar on the right.

'Sir, please save me,' pleaded Tomar while simultaneously trying to pull down Dr Gulani's trousers.

'Sir, please tell him not to hit me,' pleaded Sikarwar, tugging at his trousers.

But before the trousers could come down, Dr Gulani managed to push them away. He picked up the wooden duster from the table and charged after them. Shantanu Sikarwar ran to the left, Rajveer Tomar to the right. Dr Gulani hesitated for a moment then decided to give Shantanu the chase but couldn't keep up with his speed. Shantanu ran up the stairs of the lecture theatre two at a time and stopped at the top, waiting for

Dr Gulani to arrive, then he ran down towards the well of the theatre.

Dr Gulani gave up on him and rushed after Rajveer Tomar. They went up and down twice and when Dr Gulani started to get out of breath he stopped, took aim and threw the duster at Tomar. As expected the duster missed Tomar and hit the windowpane behind him, shattering it with a loud crash. Dr Gulani went back and stood behind the podium gasping badly. He appeared to be in urgent need of a tracheostomy, an operation performed by ENT surgeons in which a cut is made in the trachea, near the Adam's apple, to help the patient breathe.

'I am not going to take the lecture. You all think you are very smart? Well, go and read the topic from the book,' he said, still trying to catch his breath.

'Please sir, take the lecture. It's an important topic,' wailed the girls from the front rows.

'No way. I am leaving and I will report the matter to the dean,' threatened Dr Gulani. 'What is your name?' he pointed at Rajveer Tomar.

'Langad,' replied the whole class.

'It's the limit,' Dr Gulani stomped off towards the door and tried to pull it open. It didn't budge as it was locked from outside.

'Sir, you can't leave till 3 p.m., when the class will be officially over and the door will be unlocked,' shouted Mannu from the back.

'Yes sir, please stay, we want to have some more fun,' yelled Shantanu Sikarwar.

Seeing no escape route, Dr Gulani returned to the safety of the podium and ducked behind it. Someone burst a firecracker in the rear of the lecture theatre and in the closed confines, it made a big boom. The college peon came running and started to bang on the door. 'What's going on inside? Who's there in the lecture theatre?'

'Open the door!' screamed Dr Gulani from behind the podium.

'It's locked from outside, we will have to break the lock,' the peon screamed back.

Ghanshyam Prasad realized the gravity of the situation and quietly slipped out through the back door. He walked up the corridor to the main door, unlocked it and disappeared from the scene. The moment the door was opened, Dr Gulani escaped from the classroom and ran away to safety.

The first-timers attending their maiden Dr Gulani lecture couldn't believe what they had just seen and experienced. Even a lowly demonstrator commanded more respect in NMC. How did the things go so wrong for Dr Gulani? There had to be some explanation for this anomaly.

'I still can't believe it,' remarked Mehul, coming out of the lecture theatre.

'Yes, this is unbelievable,' added JD. 'Why does Dr Gulani puts up with so much ridicule?

'I'll tell you the whole story,' said Mannu Sharma, joining JD and the gang. 'It was not always like this with Dr Gulani. In fact he was quite a tyrant, especially with his postgraduate students. Then one day his senior resident, Dr Abhay Agrawal, caught him red-handed with a nurse inside his chamber. He locked them from outside and called up his wife, Dr Savita Gulani. She was attending an emergency call in the obstetrics ward and came rushing to Dr Gulani's chamber. She asked Dr Abhay Agrawal to unlock the room and dashed inside. The scene she created is still fresh in the memories of those present in the hospital at that time.'

'What exactly happened?' asked JD.

'Some say she first tore off the nurse's clothes and then beat up Dr Gulani with her sandals. Others say it was in the reverse order, but whatever the sequence, the fact is she is quite short and wears pretty high heels. The scars on Dr Gulani's forehead and face are not due to falling down the stairs, as he tells everyone, but due to falling from grace,' Mannu paused for dramatic effect.

'Then?' persisted JD.

'Then she caught hold of Dr Gulani by his collar and dragged him all the way home. This probably broke Gulani because he became the butt of jokes of the entire college right from the students to the staff. Even class-three and -four employees didn't spare him. All that you saw in the classroom hardly compares to what he went through during that phase. Although they still live together, you can well imagine what type of married life it must be...'

'This explains his diffident behaviour. I can now understand why he doesn't fight back,' said JD.

'Why doesn't he retaliate? What stops him now?' Mehul asked.

'Because he is afraid of his past. He is scared that if he hits back, people would promptly bring out the skeletons hanging in his cupboard,' analysed JD.

'Perhaps he is not half as bad as he is projected to be. In fact, he could be more decent than some other people who might be worse offenders but never get caught,' Mehul said, with pity in his voice.

'Let's forget about Dr Gulani and his past and start concentrating on the forthcoming junior final exams,' said JD, passing an arm over Mehul's shoulder.

'Yes, the exams have sneaked up so stealthily that we have been caught almost totally unawares,' agreed Mehul. 'We will have to put in at least ten to twelve hours of study every day if we just want to repeat our previous performance.'

⊕

One and a half months later, when the exams were over and the results were out, there was no major surprise. Mansi still maintained her numero uno position with JD snapping at her heels at number two. Sumit Saxena had faded off from the top ten list. Obviously his father's influence was not that strong among the teaching staff of junior final. Mehul had made substantial progress and was now at number three.

22

Gift of Life

JD's batch had now reached its final destination, that is, the senior final. Another twelve months and they would be through the MBBS course. At the moment they were in their final posting in the department of surgery. This being their last chance to pick up skill-based knowledge, most of them were attending the clinics very regularly in addition to the theory lectures.

After a week or so, Dr Rishabh Jain, associate professor of surgery, took the morning clinic. JD and the rest of the group were all eyes and ears because Dr Jain was a brilliant teacher. He was also a terrific surgeon and the daring surgeries performed by him were well known among the medical fraternity of NMC.

'Sir, Ritik, a fifteen-year-old boy with a ruptured spleen has been referred from the department of medicine to us,' spoke Rajeev Gaur, senior resident of surgery, interrupting Dr Rishabh Jain.

'Who was the consultant-in-charge of the case there?' Dr Jain questioned.

'He was admitted in Professor Vijay Khanna's unit.'

'What is the GC (General Condition) of the patient?'

'Doesn't look good.'

'Don't talk like a layman, Dr Rajeev.' Whenever Dr Jain addressed anyone with the prefix 'Dr', everyone knew he was upset with the person because otherwise he was always on first-name terms with all his postgraduates.

'Sir, he has a rapid, thready pulse with the pulse rate varying between 130 and 140.'

'BP?' snapped Dr Jain.

'The systolic is 60, I couldn't record the diastolic.'

'Where is the patient?'

'Still on the stretcher, in the admission chamber.'

'Give me the details,' said Dr Jain, walking briskly towards the admission area. Dr Rajeev Gaur was half a step behind. Most of the students dispersed but JD, Junaid, Lazarus and Mehul decided to follow them.

'The boy was playing cricket the previous evening,' began Rajeev Gaur. 'He was hit in the abdomen by the cricket ball while batting. He started to complain of pain in the abdomen after some time and left for home. When the pain didn't subside, his parents took him to a paediatrician, Dr Rakesh Kumar.'

'I know Dr Rakesh Kumar, he was my immediate senior in the medical college. He is good!' said Dr Jain.

'According to the father of the boy, Dr Kumar first wrote a prescription and asked them to come back in the morning if the pain persisted. Then he re-examined Ritik and said that he suspected there could be an internal injury and it would be better to admit the patient for observation and further investigation.'

'See? I told you Dr Kumar is good at his job! How many paediatricians would have referred a minor case of a cricket ball injury to be admitted for further evaluation?' remarked Dr Jain. 'Yes, continue...'

'The father decided that it was no big deal and instead of admitting the boy, took him home. Moreover the painkiller administered by Dr Kumar had provided some relief and Ritik was feeling better. Later in the night Ritik again developed severe pain so his father rushed him to the hospital in the middle of the night. The casualty medical officer posted there thought it to be a medical case and admitted him to the medical ward.'

'I tell you, some of these guys in the casualty are worse than traffic policemen. They send patients in all wrong directions without a proper examination,' grumbled Dr Jain.

'Ultrasonography was done about an hour earlier and it turned out that the patient has a ruptured spleen with profuse intra-abdominal bleeding. He was referred to us immediately,' Rajeev Gaur completed the narrative.

'Thank God he was in the hospital and being administered intravenous fluids and vasopressors (medicines to raise blood pressure) otherwise he would have gone into shock and collapsed,' commented Dr Jain, entering the admission area of the surgical ward.

The thin, gangly teenager lying almost unconscious on the examination table looked a deathly pale, his breathing shallow and laboured. Around him stood a middle-aged couple and an old man, most likely his parents and grandfather. Two IV lines were attached to the boy's arms, infusing plasma expanders and dopamine into his body. As Dr Jain started to examine the boy, the family retreated in the background.

'Arrange for blood urgently, the patient is sinking. We will have to operate upon him immediately or we will lose him,' barked Dr Jain, finishing his examination quickly.

'Sir, the patient's blood group is AB positive.'

'Oh, that's an uncommon blood group!' exclaimed Dr Jain.

'There are about ten to twelve people with the family standing outside the ward. I'll go and ask them to get their blood groups checked,' said Rajeev Gaur.

'Even if their blood groups don't match, request them to donate blood. We will get AB positive group blood from the blood bank in exchange,' instructed Dr Jain.

'Yes, sir,' replied Rajeev Gaur, moving away towards the corridor just outside the surgical ward.

'Put the patient on oxygen and shift him to the OT,' Dr Jain ordered the staff nurse standing beside him.

'Sir, my blood group is AB positive. Can I donate blood?' Mehul asked, coming up to Dr Jain.

'Of course you can! I appreciate your gesture, young man.' Dr Jain patted Mehul on the back. 'Ask Dr Gaur to give you a blood requisition form and go to the blood bank as soon as possible. The patient is in a precarious condition.'

'Sir, except for the parents and the grandfather, all the others disappeared the moment I asked them to get their blood group tested for donating blood,' said Rajeev Gaur disgustedly on returning from outside the ward.

'That's the usual story. The entire neighbourhood rushes to the hospital with the patient, creates chaos and hampers the functioning of the medical staff, but if you ask them to donate blood they vanish immediately,' complained Dr Jain.

'I can't understand why these people are so terrified of giving blood?' Rajeev Gaur said agitatedly.

'I use this technique all the time to clear the unwanted elements from the wards,' said Balaram, the ward boy, standing some distance away.

'Good morning, sir!' Manmohan Sharma, senior resident of surgery, greeted Dr Jain as he entered the admission area.

'Good morning, Manmohan,' said Dr Jain, leaving for his chamber.

'What's wrong with this patient?' Manmohan asked, putting down the case sheets of the patients to be discharged that morning on the table.

'He has a ruptured spleen and is in shock. We need AB positive blood urgently, at least three to four bottles during the operation and several more in the post-operative period,' answered Rajeev Gaur.

'Riyaaz Mamu is AB positive and is always willing to give blood,' informed Manmohan.

'Okay, I'll contact him if such a situation arises,' said Rajeev, filling up the blood requisition form quickly. He then sent Mehul and the parents of the boy along with the ward boy to the blood bank.

Mehul's grouping and crossmatching tests were done and on finding everything right, the blood bank technician asked Mehul to lie down on the donor couch. He applied a Velcro tourniquet to Mehul's upper arm to make the veins prominent. After cleaning the skin vigorously with a spirit swab he pushed in the needle in Mehul's vein and started to bleed him.

Fortunately, the mother of the boy turned out to be AB positive and she donated one unit of blood. The father was O positive, but he also donated blood and in exchange, the blood bank officer Dr Upendra Dwivedi issued one unit of AB positive blood. He also assured the parents that the blood bank had sufficient AB positive blood and if need be, he would issue it immediately even if there was no donor to give blood in exchange.

⊕

Dr Rishabh Jain reached the OT and was met by the senior OT nurse, Vinita.

'All set?' he asked.

'Yes sir, I have taken out the instruments needed for abdominal surgery. The three units of AB positive blood issued by the blood bank have arrived and I have already started the blood transfusion,' replied Vinita.

'Very good. Who is the anaesthetist on duty?'

'Dr Mohammad Javed.'

'Has he arrived?'

'Yes sir, he is in there checking the Boyle's apparatus (instrument used for giving general anaesthesia).'

'Ask Dr Rajeev Gaur to scrub up and be ready. I want him to assist me in the operation. And please call the parents of the patient. I want to have a word with them,' said Dr Jain, moving towards an outer chamber meant for the purpose.

Vinita ushered in the boy's parents and made them sit across the table in front of Dr Jain. Ritik's grandfather also came in and was included in the discussion.

'Ritik's condition is very grave. He has a ruptured spleen and is bleeding continuously. If we don't operate on him immediately, we will lose him. We may still lose him in spite of operating, but at least the operation gives him a chance, however slim,' spoke Dr Jain, looking directly at Ritik's father.

'You know the best, doctor sahib. We have no knowledge of these matters. Please save my child.' Ritik's father broke down in inconsolable tears.

'This is not the time to cry, this is the time to pray,' said Ritik's grandfather, coming forward and putting a comforting hand on his son's shoulder. He then looked at Dr Jain, 'Doctor sahib, last evening when Ritik went out to play, he was laughing and in high spirits. He wanted me to come to the ground and watch him hit sixes like Yuvraj. Now he is in a critical state, and as you say, he will die if an emergency operation is not performed. We have full faith in your judgment and the rest we leave to God.'

Dr Jain stood for a moment, wondering at the old man's composure. Then he glanced at Vinita, 'Get the consent papers signed and come inside the OT. I am going in to wash and change.'

At that moment JD, Junaid and Lazarus entered the room. 'Sir, can we watch the operation?'

'Of course, you can, just remove your shoes and put on OT gowns. By the way, where is Mehul?'

'Sir, he has gone to the hostel after giving blood,' replied JD.

'Okay,' said Dr Rishabh Jain and went inside the OT complex. He first went to the scrub room to disinfect himself by vigorous hand washing and then removed his outside clothes to wear a sterilized OT gown and mask. He entered the OT through an attached door and put on disposable rubber gloves.

And yes! There was no red bulb glowing outside the OT as shown in Bollywood films.

Ritik was lying on the OT table with a variety of tubes and monitoring devices attached to his body. Dr Jain nodded at Dr Mohammad Javed who quickly administered general anaesthesia to Ritik and Dr Jain started the operation. The abdominal cavity was full of blood that was leaking out of the ruptured spleen.

JD, Junaid and Lazarus watched in awe as Dr Jain's fingers flew inside Ritik's abdomen; clamping, cutting, suturing. The effect was not much different from that of watching a master musician's fingers flying over his favoured instrument at the peak of a melody. In a rapid flurry of activity he had stopped the bleeding, excised the ruptured spleen and closed the profusely bleeding spleenic artery.

The actual operation didn't last more then forty-five minutes, but it took Dr Jain another thirty minutes to close the abdomen layer by layer. He believed in leaving behind as minimal and neat a scar as possible. It was 2.30 in the afternoon when Ritik was wheeled out of the OT into the post-operative ward. He was still unconscious, his breathing laboured and his blood pressure fluctuating in the dangerous zone. Three units of blood were transfused inside the OT and the fourth was started after shifting him to the post-operative ward.

The ten-bedded post-operative ward, commonly called post-op, was like a mini ICU. All the beds were equipped with monitoring devices, central oxygen supply and suction machines. Equipment for cardioversion (giving a DC shock to restart the stopped heart) and artificial ventilation (ventilator) was also available. Residents from surgery and anaesthesia were posted in the post-op to tackle any emergency.

By evening, Ritik had already received six units of blood. Some colour had returned to his pale cheeks. Dr Rajeev Gaur and the nursing staff kept a regular check on his vitals. When Ritik's pulse and BP improved slightly, Dr Gaur went to the duty room and asked Balaram, the ward boy, to bring tea. Shantanu Sikarwar, resident of anaesthesia, dropped in to say hello and they had tea together. The dark, excessively sweet, watery brew wouldn't have been called tea at any half-decent restaurant, but it gave back some energy.

'Who's on duty tonight?' Shantanu asked, dropping the disposable cup in the dustbin.

'Manmohan, but I might come back later in the night if any emergency arises. Dr Jain is still worried about the boy whose spleen he had removed this afternoon. The patient has lost quite a lot of blood and is still not out of shock.'

'Yes, he appears quite bad still,' agreed Shantanu.

'We have received four more units of blood from the blood bank which we are going to infuse during the night. Let's hope he comes out of it,' sighed Rajeev Gaur, slumping down in the chair.

'He will,' assured Shantanu before leaving.

Manmohan came on duty at 8.30 p.m. and after taking the round of the post-op ward, settled down in the duty room with *Schwartz's Principles of Surgery*. Around midnight, the ward nurse tapped sharply on the door of the duty room. 'Doctor, please come quickly, Ritik has collapsed.'

Manmohan rushed out of the duty room towards the post-op ward. Ritik's pulse was very feeble and the BP was fluctuating between low and very low. This meant that he was going into cardiac decompensation. Simply speaking, his heart was not pumping properly. The abdominal distension was still present, hampering the movements of the diaphragm and leading to shallow rapid breathing.

'Send an urgent call to Dr Jain and start a norad (noradrenaline) drip,' Dr Manmohan Sharma instructed the nurse. He glanced at the monitor attached to Ritik. It showed a heart rate of 160, the systolic blood pressure was 40 mm of Hg and the oxygen saturation just 60 per cent. He increased the oxygen flow and readjusted the rate of the dopamine drip that had been going on right from the time Ritik was admitted to the ward. He increased it by almost 25 per cent in the hope that the drug would help in sustaining Ritik's BP. By the time Dr Jain arrived, Ritik's BP and respiration had stabilized and his oxygen saturation had gone up to 86 per cent.

'Good job, Manmohan, just maintain his BP and respiration. He should come out of it by morning,' said Dr Jain with confidence.

'Yes, sir,' uttered Manmohan with obvious pride.

'Send a call to the anaesthetist on duty and put the patient on CPAP (Continuous Positive Airway Pressure).'

'Okay, sir.'

Throughout the night, Ritik's condition remained critical. Twice his BP sunk so low that Dr Manmohan Sharma had to literally pump medicines into his system to tide over the crisis. By 7 a.m., Ritik's breathing became less laboured, his oxygen saturation went up to 94, his heart rate went down to a more manageable 130 and his BP became a steady 80/50 mm of Hg.

Ritik regained consciousness in the afternoon. Gradually, his vitals normalized further and one-by-one the life-saving equipment was slowly disconnected from his body. Within a span of twenty-four hours, he had received ten units of blood, several life-saving drugs, newer expensive antibiotics and above all, dedicated critical care. If he was alive, it was thanks to a team of devoted doctors. It was due to them that death lurking in the hospital corridors had to return empty-handed.

Ritik was discharged on the seventh day from the confines of the hospital. There was a big smile on his grandfather's face. His parents were ecstatic and went up to Dr Jain and tried to touch his feet. Dr Jain patted them affectionately. Ritik was wearing new clothes, his shoes were new, he was sporting a brand-new funky looking wristwatch, but what was more important was he owned a new, charmed life. He would receive many gifts in life, but the gift of life would always remain the most important.

⊕

'I wanted to tell you about the patient you referred to us a week back,' Dr Rishabh Jain told Dr Rakesh Kumar during an IMA (Indian Medical Association) meeting. 'You saved that boy, Ritik, by referring him for admission.'

'Which one?' Dr Kumar was unable to place the patient.

'The one with the cricket ball injury in the abdomen.'

'Oh, I remember now! In fact, I was going to send him back to his home after prescribing painkillers. But something about his look troubled me and I decided to refer him to the hospital. You can say it was a split-second decision. What was the exact diagnosis?' asked Dr Kumar.

'He had a ruptured spleen. We had to operate on him to remove it and it took ten bottles of blood to save him,' replied Dr Jain.

Dr Kumar put his arm on Dr Jain's shoulder. No words were exchanged, none were needed, as two life-saviours savoured their victory over death.

23
The Final Hurdle

During their final rotation in the department of medicine, JD's batch was sent on a two weeks' posting to the medicine outpatient department (commonly known as OPD). Long queues of male and female patients formed at the registration counter daily at 8 a.m. By 8.30 they got restless, by 9 abusive and by 9.30 combative, usually the time when junior doctors arrived. The registration clerk only started to make OPD slips after the arrival of the doctors.

As far as senior consultants were concerned, they arrived and departed at any time convenient to them. They were always very busy attending to VIPs, because if you wanted to remain in NMC, Bhopla, you had to 'set' one or two high and mighty bureaucrats or politicians and keep them in good humour through personalized care and home visits. In the remaining time, the consultants looked after the welfare of their private patients. Hence, despite their best efforts and most noble intentions they missed out on serving humanity at large.

The medicine OPD, located on the second floor of the new OPD block, consisted of a large central hall with a registration counter and a series of small chambers for the junior doctors and consultants. The walls had ceramic tiles up to a height of six feet. The few tiles in the upper parts, out of the spitting range of Bhoplaites, still retained their original white colour. The rest had turned red or maroon, depending on the mixture of chuna and kathaa in the spit.

The hall had a few metal benches and some plastic bucket seats attached to metal frames. The only plentiful feature was the plethora of health ministry posters pasted haphazardly on the walls. They warned the people against spitting, coughing and indiscriminate sex, while exhorting them to eat nutritious diet, rich in iron, calcium and proteins—without actually telling them how to arrange the finances for it. No bank would ever sanction a loan for eating a well-balanced diet.

The doctors' chambers were crammed, crummy, stuffy and dark. The only furniture was a doctor's desk and chair, one examination table and a stool. Meant for the patient to sit upon, the stool was tied to the leg of the examination table by bandages. This prevented the patient from getting too chummy with the doctor. It also protected the doctor from the tobacco, onion, garlic, salan and sweat fumes emanating from the patient.

After failing to move the stool by the time the patient opened his mouth to describe his complaints, the doctor handed him his prescription, which he had quickly scribbled while the patient was struggling with the stool. Due to a government ruling, the doctor couldn't prescribe medicines from outside and hardly any were available in the hospital, so doctors had stopped listening to the complaints of the patients. What's the use, they said, when ultimately you are going to write the same four medicines?

TC—Tetracycline
PC—Paracetamol
BC—B-Complex
MV—Multivitamin

There was another problem with the government's circular forcing doctors to write only hospital medicines. The quality of the drugs was such that most patients failed to show any improvement. This resulted in their losing confidence in the government doctors' abilities.

The most common complaint in the OPD was headache, closely followed by gas, constipation, chakkar, backache and insomnia. The insomniacs' usual complaint was that they have not slept even for a second in the last twenty years. Most of the symptoms were clearly incompatible with normal life if they had actually existed. The doctors of NMC, Bhopla, were quite adept at such games. First, they made the patient go around the entire length and breadth of the hospital campus getting X-rays, ultrasonography and blood tests done. After all, every patient must be investigated thoroughly in case something really sinister had given cause for complaint! Then whether the reports were normal or abnormal, they packed off the patient to some other department. Most of the doctors would have easily overshadowed Pele in a game of football. They were experts at kicking the patients around dexterously and would surely have outperformed the legendary football star on the football field.

A persistent patient with an intractable headache could easily be referred to the eye department with a quick scribble of the free pen provided by some pharma company. After the eye department had found nothing and were tired of the fellow appearing in their field of vision week after week, they sent him to Dr Gulani's ENT OPD.

Dr Gulani usually operated on all his patients and generally removed their tonsils or punctured their sinuses. When the patient continued to attend the ENT OPD with recurring headaches, his junior doctors would pack him off to the surgical OPD with the provisional diagnosis that his headache was the result of a hidden sepsis in his liver, gall bladder, kidney or some other organ conveniently outside their domain.

The surgeons might or might not operate on the patient, depending upon the length of their waiting list at the time. Whatever happened, after a few more visits to the surgical OPD, the patient found himself in the dental section having most of his teeth pulled out by fresh practitioners of the art.

The lucky few went on to the department of neurology where after several aborted attempts they finally could lie down and take a nap on the CT-scan table. Not even Bill Gates can afford a two-crore bed to sleep upon. When the poor-quality scan failed to show any abnormality and the headaches persisted, the neurologist as a last resort referred the patient to the psychiatrist. The psychiatrist was then unable to transfer the patient to anyone and the patient continued to visit him and discuss his headaches once a month for the remainder of his life.

One morning, JD, Junaid, Mehul, Mansi and Minal were whiling away time waiting for the resident doctors and, hopefully, the consultants to arrive. It was already ten o'clock, well past the official timing of 8 a.m. and the medical OPD was teeming with patients who were getting impatient by the minute.

'When will doctor sahib come?' asked an old lady, touching Minal's arm.

'Very soon,' answered Minal doubtingly.

'What is wrong with you, Amma?' Mehul ventured.

'That's the trouble—they don't know what's wrong with me. I was admitted in the surgical ward for two months with pain in my abdomen. First they removed my gall bladder, then when the pain didn't subside, they opened me up again and took out my appendix along with some of my intestines. I am lucky to be standing here talking to you.'

'You are in the wrong place, this is the medical OPD,' informed Minal.

'I know this hospital like the back of my hand. I've been

referred by Dr P. R. Tripathi, the chief surgeon, to the medical OPD,' said the old lady smugly.

At that moment, the two resident doctors arrived and in the ensuing commotion, the old lady disappeared from their side.

'Hey, let's go to the emergency,' said Junaid. 'I have befriended Mohammad Ismail, the senior compounder. He will let us apply stitches and give injections.'

Everyone agreed immediately as it was far more exciting to sew up wounds and inject drugs into patients' bums than listening to the same old complaints standing in a crowded, stuffy, smelly OPD room.

⊕

One evening, while returning from a movie, JD reminded the gang, 'Do you guys realize it is exactly eight weeks today to our final exam?'

'What!' Junaid stopped in his tracks. 'It can't be. They are not going to be held till the end of March.'

'Well, this is the end of January.'

'If we don't start studying really hard, it will be the end of us,' cried Manish and Lazarus. They knew it very well that, academically, JD and Mehul belonged to a different category altogether.

So the preparations for the final examination began in right earnest. JD, Junaid, Lazarus, Mehul and Manish went to the college library and dug out the file containing the question papers of the past ten years. They carefully went through the questions and prepared a detailed list of the most frequently asked questions subject-wise. They also noted the year in which that question had been asked.

'It's no good wasting time on tuberculosis, diabetes and hypertension,' declared Junaid after scrutinizing the medicine papers. 'They were asked the last time. I think it's not worth learning about pneumonia either, its been there for the past three years.'

'There is an old dictum: know something about everything and everything about some things,' said JD. 'Going by that rule, we should not overlook these diseases completely.'

'Where is the time, yaar? We won't be able to finish the course even once,' argued Junaid.

'Yes, we can leave them safely,' seconded Manish. 'Dr Vijay Khanna is very fond of rare diseases and syndromes. According to the seniors, his favourites are brucellosis, Q fever, the Brown-Séquard syndrome, Charcot-Marie-Tooth disease, the Lennox-Gastaut syndrome, the Ramsay Hunt syndrome and Saint Vitus's dance,' said Mehul, reading from a list he had prepared.

'Well, some of them appear pretty straightforward,' remarked Lazarus with a straight face. 'Q fever is caused by standing in a queue for too long. It is very common in our country because we have long queues for practically everything. Even for burials!'

'The Ramsay Hunt syndrome should be even simpler,' Manish joined in the fun. 'It is the syndrome you develop when you watch too many horror movies made by the Ramsay Brothers.'

'When a saint is in the mood to shake a leg with nuns, it is called Saint Vitus's dance,' added Junaid, doubling up with laughter.

'Okay, enough is enough!' Mehul tried to restore order. 'I think we should study brucellosis, Q fever, the Brown-Séquard syndrome and the Lennox-Gastaut syndrome in detail,' he said decisively.

'All right, I will look them up in Davidson's textbook of medicine and prepare notes for you,' assured JD with sincerity, though he secretly knew that these rare diseases would never figure in the exams.

JD had learnt from his seniors that it was highly unlikely that they would ever come across a case of these rare diseases and syndromes after doing their MBBS. And even if they would, there was every chance that they wouldn't be able to recognize them! But he did know, with the astuteness of a topper, that to be well prepared about brucellosis, Q fever, the Brown-Séquard syndrome and the Lennox-Gastaut syndrome, might well be the difference between merely passing and topping in the upcoming exams.

The game of one-upmanship was full on during dinnertime in the mess. The most commonly adopted tactics to depress the enemy (competitor) were to innocently ask, 'Hey, have you read about Chagas disease?' or, 'What is the treatment of Rocky Mountain spotted fever?' The guy would rush back to his room immediately after finishing dinner to start mugging the obscure disease, thereby wasting his time on something that probably would never be asked in the exams.

The examination was divided into two parts: theory papers and clinical assessment including the grand viva. The candidate had to pass both separately. While most students were able to write something or the other in theory papers, it was the clinical exam which proved their nemesis. With the examiner breathing fire like a dragon down their necks they had to not only make a competent diagnosis, but also convince the dragon about it.

The theory papers began on a bright, sunny morning with medicine being the first subject. One glance at the question paper and the morning turned grey and gloomy for most students because they had adopted the same tactics as Junaid, Lazarus and Manish. They had left out the topics covered in the previous year's papers.

'Describe the management of tuberculosis with special emphasis on DOT'—was the first question. 'Give a detailed account of the complications of diabetes'—was the second. The students cursed in disgust. They felt the examiners had played a really dirty trick by repeating not one but two of the previous year's questions.

Junaid glanced at JD, who was already busy writing furiously. His eyes met Manish, who shrugged his shoulders helplessly. Junaid somehow filled up three pages on the management of tuberculosis but he had absolutely no clue about what DOT meant. Could it be Death On Table? But why would a TB patient die on the table, since that honour usually goes to surgical cases. Could it be Department of Telecommunication? But Junaid couldn't think of any link between tuberculosis and telecommunication. Moreover, the 2G (scam) and TB didn't rhyme that well. The poor fellow hadn't bothered to acquaint himself with the new national health programmes. If he had, he would have surely known what DOT in relation to tuberculosis meant.

Junaid was sweating heavily when he came to the second question. He had left diabetes altogether but he knew a lot about obesity, which he had mugged the whole night. What the heck! he thought, and started to scribble rapidly, 'Diabetes is a complication of obesity, now we will discuss the complications of obesity.' He ended up filling ten pages.

Coming out of the examination hall after the paper was over, Junaid asked JD, 'What does DOT stand for?'

'It is an abbreviation for Directly Observed Therapy. DOT has been launched to improve patient compliance. In this programme, a trained healthcare worker provides the prescribed TB drugs and watches the patient swallow every dose. Thus most of the patients who otherwise wouldn't have completed the full course of anti-tubercular medicines complete the entire treatment,' replied JD.

'Thank God! I didn't write Death On Table,' Junaid blurted out.

✦

The cases (patients) for clinical examinations are generally collected from the wards and OPD. A few of them are old stalwarts who are registered with various departments and are called in during the examinations. They end up attending so many exams that they know a whole lot about their illness in addition to several medical terms. Some bright chaps are more knowledgeable about their illness than those examining them.

JD, Junaid, Lazarus, Manish and Mehul stood in a huddle just outside the medicine ward, waiting to be called in. Riyaaz Mamu joined them holding a small white slip in his hand. He was appearing for the fifth time in the medicine exam and was taking no chances on this occasion. One of the resident medical officers had provided him a list of cases picked up by the examiners and the small white slip in his hand contained that information.

'There is an asthma patient in a green shirt,' informed Riyaaz Mamu, reading from the list. 'A teenage girl with an enlarged liver and spleen is just by the side of the door as you enter.'

Everybody made a mental note of it.

'Then there's a little boy with nephrotic syndrome—his body is all bloated up. A young woman with mitral stenosis due to rheumatic fever is on the corner bed. And...'

At that precise moment, the door opened and all of them were asked to get inside. One half of the ward was cordoned off by screens and patients were scattered on beds, wheelchairs and examination tables. The scene could well have been from any Indian airport lounge after a cancelled Air India flight. In one corner across a large desk sat the examiners sipping coffee. Strong coffee for examiners is a must during all medical examinations. Without it the examiners are highly likely to doze off as they are bored to death asking the same questions and listening to the same blunders.

Lazarus was directed to a dour-faced examiner with a

perpetually grumpy expression on his face. 'Good morning, sir,' he wished him pleasantly.

The examiner looked at Lazarus as if he was disappointed to see him. He asked a few questions and every answer Lazarus made was received with the same grim and grouchy look. Lazarus found it very unnerving but couldn't do anything about it.

'Go and examine that young woman on the corner bed. I'll be with you in thirty minutes.'

Lazarus reached the corner bed and stood smiling apologetically at the young woman. She smiled back brightly. Gaining in confidence Lazarus took out his pen and a sheaf of papers. 'What is your name?' he asked.

'My name is Sunita Singh. I am twenty-three, unmarried and I work as a computer operator in a private firm. I live in Buddha Nagar with my parents and I have one elder brother.'

Lazarus relaxed: she knew the format of history-taking quite well. 'How long have you been coming to the examinations?' he asked. 'You seem to know all the questions beforehand.'

'Since childhood,' Sunita laughed.

Lazarus was maha pleased. Getting an educated patient in the examinations was like hitting the jackpot. In all probability she was net-savvy and would know quite a bit about her illness. All he had to do was play his cards correctly. He talked to her about her interests, hobbies, films she liked, the malls she frequented and whether she had any boyfriend (which elicited shy giggles). He cautioned her to take proper care while working on the computer. 'It can cause backache and eye strain,' he told her with deep concern.

'Thanks for the advice. I'll be more cautious now onwards.'

'By the way,' Lazarus said casually, 'what's wrong with you?'

'I knew it was coming. I have been instructed not to disclose my diagnosis but you are such a nice person that I will break my promise for you. I have mitral stenosis due to rheumatic fever but my heart is in perfect shape and I have a favourable prognosis.'

'Please let me know the details, if any,' spoke Lazarus jotting down the information frantically.

'There's a pre-systolic murmur at the apex but the pulmonary and aortic areas are clear. I am perfectly well compensated and there is no lung congestion. So if the examiner asks are there any crepts (crepitation or crackling sounds) at the bases of my lungs, say "No".'

'Okay. Thanks a lot,' Lazarus noted down the description hurriedly.

The dour-faced examiner lost his perpetually grumpy expression when Lazarus told him the accurate diagnosis.

'Very good!' He smiled for the first time, lifting the clouds of gloom from his otherwise pleasant face. 'Are there any creps at the bases of the lungs?'

'No, sir.'

'Correct again! I am really very impressed. Some of you young fellows do have a keen clinical sense.'

'Thank you, sir,' Lazarus said gracefully.

'Now take a look at this ECG and let me know what you think about it.' The examiner opened a folder he was carrying and pointed towards it. Several paper strips with squiggly lines covered the entire sheet. Lazarus felt exactly like the dyslexic kid in the movie *Taare Zameen Par*. The time had come for some quick thinking. Looking intently at the ECG strips, Lazarus let out a long whistle of amazement.

'Yes, it's the tracing of a patient with ventricular fibrillation, isn't it?' The examiner said, happily taking away the ECG folder and patting Lazarus on the back.

From the corner of his eyes Lazarus saw the examiner make a double tick against his name on the mark sheet. With a respectful bow towards the examiner and a grateful smile at Sunita he escaped from the ward on a trot.

⊕

During the ObG practical exam, Manish lost his nerve in front of the examiners. Confusion breeds confusion and soon he came to the end of his interrogation struggling like a Nano in a traffic snarl surrounded by Safaris and Scorpios.

One of the examiners finally decided to try the poor fellow with something different and asked him to conduct a mock delivery. There was a life-size plastic model of the lower half of the female trunk, into which a rubber mannequin the size of a newborn baby was placed from the top.

'Don't be nervous,' said the examiner. This made an already nervous Manish completely jittery.

'Now this is Mrs Mittal during her first delivery,' the examiner pointed towards the female trunk. 'The labour is prolonged and the baby is not coming out on its own. You have decided to conduct a forceps delivery. Show me the steps in an orderly manner,' instructed the examiner, providing Manish with a pair of obstetrical forceps.

With shaking hands, Manish introduced the forceps in the pelvis and applied the two blades of the forceps to the head of the baby, taking care to put the correct one on first. He locked the handle, took it in the approved grip and gave a gentle tug. Nothing happened. He pulled harder, but the baby refused to come out. His mouth went dry and his heartbeat became irregular. He started to sweat profusely as he saw his chances of passing fade like an Abhishek Bachchan movie. Manish gave a last desperate heave. His feet slipped and he fell on the floor and over his head flew the forceps.

The examiner stared at him as he struggled to get up from

the floor. Then he caught him by his collar and yanked him up. 'Now go and break the good news to Mr Mittal that he can remarry and start a new family since you have wiped out the previous one, you maniac!'

24
Love Comes Second Best

There is usually some breathing space between the end of the senior final exams and the beginning of internship. Making use of this brief hiatus, most of the students had rushed to their homes for a well-deserved rest before the grind began again. Without the completion of one year's internship, the MBBS degree is not awarded. During this one year, the students are posted in various departments for varying lengths of time. They are supposed to learn the basic skills of each medical specialty in these postings.

With the introduction of the pre-PG (postgraduation) test this essential component of medical training has been all but lost. Now instead of working in the hospital wards and picking up clinical skills, students remain closeted in their rooms mugging up MCQs (Multiple Choice Questions) for clearing the pre-PG test. If a student clears the test, well and good, he or she at least gets admission into a postgraduate course decided not by choice but by rank. The problem arises when the person is unable to get a PG seat, which is the fate of more than 60 per cent students. Thanks to the short-sightedness of the government, the PG seats are very limited. When a plain MBBS doctor is faced with the prospect of examining a patient, he hardly knows where to begin and where to end. He fumbles and flounders his way through the patients like a blind mouse in a maze. Gradually, he develops the necessary skills to deal with the day-to-day health problems of the patients but with several mishaps in between.

The results of the senior final exam were out after a fortnight. Finally, JD topped the merit list, Mansi was second, Minal third and in between were some new faces. Mehul had been pushed down to the seventh rank. After the introduction of the pre-PG exam—the exam that has to be cleared before one gets a PG seat—these ranks have become largely academic. You may be the topper of your batch, but if you don't get through the pre-PG exam, you are doomed. This generally doesn't happen. If you are good, you are good and you perform well in all exams. But then who can predict illness or some other such misfortune? Your hard work during the five years of the MBBS course then amounts to a big zero.

JD felt more vindicated than elated with the results. He always knew that he had the capability to top, it was just a matter of things falling into place at the right time. He did spare a thought for Mansi, she must be feeling a bit low, probably a tad dejected but then that's life. The sooner one learns to cope with setbacks the faster one comes up trumps.

In fact, Mansi was quite a lot in his thoughts. Since the final exams, their contact had diminished considerably as everybody was busy preparing for the pre-PG exams. Mansi hardly attended the ward postings; even JD spent less time in the hospital and more in the library or his room studying. These were the crucial months that could make or break his career. Getting a good rank in the pre-PG exam was on everybody's mind right now.

Sitting in the library, JD closed the book he was reading and leaned back in his chair. This morning his emotions were in turmoil. He had a feeling that Mansi was avoiding him deliberately. She had not responded to his SMS the previous evening asking her to come to the library. But then she was never very particular about replying to his SMSs. He decided to go to the hostel in the evening to meet her. He wanted to confront her with the question he had been waiting to ask for ages: 'Do you love me?' He needed to know whether they had any future together and he prayed for the response to be in the affirmative.

JD had been studying since morning, so when his tired eyes closed, he dozed off. 'What if she says a quick no or takes too long to decide?' A strange voice in his mind asked, 'Well, I'll tell her that most of the things we miss in life are due to saying no too soon or yes too late,' replied JD in his dream.

He kept hanging between hope and despair, dreams and lucidity, happiness and remorse.

'Hey JD, wake up,' Mansi stood by his side, shaking him by his shoulder.

JD opened his eyes and saw the girl he was dreaming about standing in front of him. His heart gave a lurch and stopped and then it galloped away rapidly.

'So, this is how you prepare for the pre-PG exam,' Mansi laughed.

A thousand brilliant suns lit up the sky and a million little bells tinkled in the gentle breeze that had started to blow suddenly.

'Oh, come sit down. So you got my SMS.' JD sat up in his chair.

'Yes,' said Mansi briefly, putting down the book she was carrying on the table.

'Why are you reading the PLAB (Professional and Linguistic Assessment Board of UK) guide?' JD asked, looking carefully at Mansi's book.

'Why would one read a PLAB guide? Obviously, to clear the PLAB exam, which is essential for foreign medical graduates to gain entry into England,' answered Mansi coolly.

'So you are planning to go to England?' JD was a bit taken aback for he could not remember Mansi mentioning this to him.

'No, I am not planning to go to England. I *am* going to England.'

'But I am not giving PLAB. I have no intention of going to the UK.' JD's voice had acquired a slight edge.

'What can I say about you? I can't force you.'

'It's not about you or me, stupid. It's about us.'

'That's why I have come here. To talk about us.' Mansi breathed in slowly.

'Yes, I am listening.'

'JD, you are a nice guy. I really like you.'

'So what's the problem? You know how I feel about you.'

'Please let me complete what I'm saying. It is not easy for me coming here and telling you that I am going away. Not on a vacation but on a long journey. I don't know when I will be back or if at all,' Mansi's face looked grim but determined.

JD sat back stunned. He kept looking at Mansi's face for some clue, for some respite, for a lifeline. He hoped that all this was a bad dream and very soon he would wake up and the bad spell would be broken. But nothing of that sort happened, as Mansi started to speak again.

'I am going to England after completing my internship. I know I'll clear the PLAB. The Tanejas, our very old family friends, are settled in Birmingham. Mr Taneja is a GP (general practitioner). His son Vishal will be awarded his FRCS soon. I am getting engaged to Vishal in a short while.'

JD looked stunned, as if lightning, thunderbolts and electric currents had struck him simultaneously. More fool him for believing in happy endings.

'So you are going to marry a guy you hardly know,' JD spoke, his tone laced with bitterness.

'Five years ago, even you were a stranger to me.' Mansi's eyes slithered away.

'But now that you know me, you are still leaving me for a guy you don't know or might never really know or love.'

'JD, please don't make it difficult for me. We never had a commitment between us and I have seen even committed relationships break.'

'It is easy for you to say that now, but I was always committed to you.'

'I don't know, but it is not you I am leaving. It is the system that I am escaping from. After spending two to three years in preparation for the PMT, the entrance test, and five years in passing the MBBS, what do you get? Five thousand bucks a month! That works out to a princely sum of ₹ 60,000 per year. Compare that to any engineering student. Even a pass-out from a third-rate college of dubious standard ends up with a package of three to five lakhs per annum. That, too, after putting in just four years of mild mental exercise.'

'You can't compare the two. These are very different career options,' said JD.

'I am not doing anything of that sort. But can't you see the dice is loaded in favour of one and patently unjust to the other? It means there is something rotten in our system.'

'But that's hardly my fault.'

'I am not saying that it's your fault, but you are willing to be a part of that faulty system, I am not. The problem doesn't end here, it's actually the beginning. After putting in six years of hard labour, your future is still uncertain. You don't know whether you will get through the pre-PG exam. Even if you clear it, whether you will get the subject of your choice or not. And I have not said anything about the place you may end up doing your PG from. You might get Delhi or you may end up at Jhumri Talaiyya.'

JD smiled in spite of himself. 'One of my true-blue Punjabi, butter chicken crazy cousins did his MD from Chennai and he still gets nightmares that he is drowning in a pool of rasam.'

Mansi laughed her tinkling laugh and it killed JD instantly. Whatever the circumstances, she continued to have the same effect on JD's emotions.

Getting serious once again, Mansi looked searchingly at JD's face. She could see some pain, some sadness but she could also detect a grim determination setting in. 'During postgraduation, again you will be exploited. You'll be paid peanuts and in the name of tuition fees, the government will shamelessly steal from it. The amount of work the postgraduates do and the money they get for it has absolutely no correlation.'

'Yes, the entire workload of the medical college hospitals is taken care of by the PGs,' agreed JD willingly.

'By the time you pass your MD exam, you are approaching thirty and what is your worth? Probably 25,000 bucks a month! With the present rate of inflation, you will still be riding your motorbike and dreaming of an Alto. The government would screw you further by sending you to a remote village because they had forced you into signing a bond with them.'

JD realized that every single word of Mansi was true. He too felt that it was only doctors who were expected to fulfil their moral responsibilities. Why did no one ask the IIT and IIM graduates to chip in for the betterment of villages and villagers?

'I am not a sucker to fall for this gross exploitation in the name of humanity. If it is not immoral for an IIM graduate to work for a multinational company, it is also moral for a MBBS to go abroad to work in a foreign country. By going abroad I'll be able to lead a life I desire and deserve. When you will still be struggling to fill your motorbike's petrol tank, I'll be driving a BMW. Even if I am posted in a village, there would be electricity, roads and above all, a well-equipped hospital to work in. I'll be able to breathe clean, fresh air and deal with honest, upright people.' While putting forth her argument, unknowingly Mansi's voice had risen many a decibel and several boys and girls started to look in her direction.

'You are a very good person, JD, and I admire several qualities in you,' Mansi said, ignoring the stares. She put her hand lightly over JD's, 'I know you will prove to be a great doctor. It is my personal belief that only a good human being can be a good doctor.'

With these final parting words, Mansi stood up and was gone. She didn't look back even once and JD didn't say 'palat' once. It was not a Shah Rukh Khan movie in slow motion. It was life in fast forward.

⊕

JD came back to his hot, humid room and lay down on his unmade bed. The bedsheet had not been changed for a fortnight but he didn't care. Right from his childhood he had always wanted to be a doctor, but now that he was on the verge of being one he was not so sure. What Mansi had said made him realize that instead of being happy he was actually confused, also a bit afraid at the prospect of becoming a doctor. For the past several months he had been mugging endlessly for the pre-PG exam. He had hardly bothered to visit the wards. Yes, he knew which gene is affected in MSUD (Maple Syrup Urine Disease), but he didn't know how to treat a simple case of urinary tract infection. He knew about the DNA amplification technique to produce the DNA recombinant hepatitis-B vaccine, but he had no clue what to do if he came across a case of jaundice. Was it a travesty of fate or a tragedy of the system? He had no answers.

He reminisced about his friend Karan whom he used to teach during their school days. Karan was never in the merit list while JD always topped it. Now after six years, he was lying on an unkempt bed earning five thousand bucks a month and still hitting his head against thick tomes, while Karan commanded a cool 9.5 lakh package in a software firm, stayed in starred hotels and travelled by air, earning frequent-flyer points. He went into a fitful sleep full of demons of the past, present and the future.

Time is a great healer, friends the best balm and work the ultimate tranquillizer. JD gradually overcame the trauma but Mansi remained embedded in his LAD (Left Anterior Descending, the main coronary artery) like a big atherosclerotic plaque. She gave him heartache from time to time but he liked the pain. At least something of hers was still intact inside him. He was grateful to Mansi for hurting him with the truth instead of comforting him with a lie.

25
Not All Affairs End in Heartbreak

JD, Mehul and Lazarus were sitting on the parapet of the hostel roof gossiping. Since the Mansi episode, Lazarus had practically shifted in with JD and Mehul in their room. His jovial presence acted as a very effective shock absorber while Mehul could always be counted upon for solid emotional support. They had been studying the entire evening and had come up to the roof after dinner for some fresh air.

'I am totally freaked out, I think I can't study any more tonight,' said JD.

'Yes, even I am bored to death,' added Mehul.

'Then let me tell you a new joke that I have just received from a friend,' said Lazarus.

'Please, not one of your potty jokes again,' JD chided Lazarus.

'I can't help it, all my thoughts revolve around that theme but it's a nice one.'

'Okay, let's suffer it,' said Mehul.

'Well!' began Lazarus. 'An American, a Japanese and dear Santa were sitting in a sauna naked. There was a beeping sound. The American pressed his forearm and the beeping stopped. "That's my pager," he said. "I have a microchip under the skin of my forearm." A phone rang. The Japanese lifted his palm to his ear. "That's my mobile phone. I have a microchip in my hand." Santa felt low-tech and inferior. He didn't know what to do, so he decided to take a break in the toilet. Upon returning, he didn't realize that a piece of toilet paper had got stuck between his buttocks and was hanging from his bum. The others asked, "What is that?" Santa looked back and explained, "Oh, I am receiving a FAX!" The American and the Japanese fainted.'

JD and Mehul doubled up with laughter.

'What's so funny?' Prem Arora asked, appearing on the rooftop suddenly.

'Lazarus was telling us a joke,' JD said, shaking hands with Prem. 'What's up?' he asked casually.

'I am sure you will be shocked to hear the news.' Prem smiled with a superior air.

'Then shock us,' Lazarus looked up at Prem.

'I have got engaged to Ragini Ratra. We are getting married next month.'

There was a small pause before Lazarus commented mockingly, 'So, finally someone has fallen for you.'

'As a matter of fact, I've fallen for her,' said Prem, ignoring Lazarus's jibe.

'That's nothing new, you have been falling for every girl on the NMC campus,' Lazarus continued to throw stinging punches.

'I am so happy at the moment that I won't take offence, however hard you try,' said Prem, sitting down beside JD.

'How did it all happen?' asked JD.

'You remember the carnival night when I proposed to Ragini? How she accepted and then I played dirty?'

'Yes, I remember it vividly. You wanted an escape route and Riyaaz Mamu advised you to propose to as many girls as you could get hold of, so it all became a big joke.'

'For several days after the incident, I kept thinking that I was a mean bastard. I had no right to hurt such a sweet girl like Ragini.'

'She has to be sweet to accept you after what you did to

her,' Mehul who had been silent all this while spoke acerbically.

'I thought about that incident continuously. I realized Ragini must really like me to have said yes so spontaneously. In fact she was the only girl who accepted me so naturally,' Prem became quiet suddenly.

'So what did you do to rekindle the fire again?' JD prodded.

'Slowly, the realization dawned on me that I liked a lot of things about Ragini, her smile, her grace, her poise and above all, her calm persona. One day we met in the library and got talking. I said sorry to her and she accepted my apology gracefully. While talking to her I felt so much at peace, so happy that I didn't want to leave. After that, we kept meeting regularly and then a few days back I proposed to her again,' Prem paused for effect.

'This time you were sober and not drunk like on the previous occasion,' joked JD.

'Yes I was absolutely sober and dead serious too.'

'So what did she say?' JD asked.

'She asked, "Are you sure you want to spend the rest of your life with me?" And I said, "Yes, I do." She took my hand in hers and we sealed our relationship with a kiss.'

The rooftop was suddenly bathed in a soft, silky whiteness as the moon came out from behind a cluster of dark clouds. JD saw Prem's radiant face as he smiled at him. He leaned towards his friend and gave him a warm hug. Prem hugged him back tightly, not letting him go for a long time.

Everyone was happy for Prem—so what if FOSLA had lost its president!

⊕

Acknowledgements

Thank You All!

I was introduced to the acronym FOSLA by my wife Neelkamal Kapoor. It remained embedded at the back of my mind for several years till one fine morning on the way to my clinic I decided to write a book with the same title. Many thoughts, several ideas and plenty of anecdotes flew back and forth between us. We agreed on some and rejected some till finally a basic framework emerged. Then on, as the story progressed, I kept going back to her not only for hard facts (she being a medical teacher) but also to confirm and comprehend female responses and behaviour in several situations presented in this book. A big thank you from the apex of my heart (bottom of the heart sounds so clichéd).

A special thank you is reserved for Kausalya Saptharishi of Rupa Publications for believing in the book and working tirelessly to bring it in its present shape. Sincere thanks are due to Kapish Mehra, MD Rupa Publications, for always being so supportive.

I must thank Anvika Kapoor, Avanee Kapoor, Prateek Shah, Manoj Tandon, Chhavi Tandon, Mohammad Ali Husainy, Bindu Gurtoo and Ranjana Tandon for going through the initial drafts and coming up with useful inputs.

There is a long list of friends who have complicated as well as complimented my life. I would have liked to name them but the fear of retribution by those who would have been left out inadvertently made me decide that it's safer not to mention any. I understand that they will understand.

www.ingramcontent.com/pod-product-compliance
Lightning Source LLC
Chambersburg PA
CBHW020608270326
41927CB00005B/232